HITTING DRILLS

and

MUCH MORE

HITTING DRILLS

and

MUCH MORE

ROBERT M. BRAUN, SR.

HITTING DRILLS AND MUCH MORE

Edited by Mary Maffei

iUniverse books may be ordered through booksellers or by contacting:

iUniverse
1663 Liberty Drive
Bloomington, IN 47403
www.iuniverse.com
844-349-9409

ISBN: 978-1-6632-1859-9 (sc)
ISBN: 978-1-6632-1858-2 (e)

Library of Congress Control Number: 2021903269

Print information available on the last page.

iUniverse rev. date: 02/17/2021

This Book Belongs To: _____

Cover By D. Braun

On Deck (1993, color pencil, 10" × 14")

On Deck is a young baseball player waiting for his time to hit. With the sharp edges of the dugout in the background and the fence in front, the on-deck hitter stands out. At this moment, a hitter must have confidence in himself. Confidence comes from working hard and smart.

To our children and grandchildren.

CONTENTS

INTRODUCTION

This hitting drill manual is designed to help correct many common hitting mistakes such as stepping in the bucket and casting. It also provides valuable information regarding the development and management of ballplayers, such as the simple task of choosing the right bat, the ultimate ingredients for hitting success, and hitting drills. It is simple enough for a new player and is sophisticated enough for the most advanced player. It is a usable tool for the first-year coach and for the seasoned veteran. Everyone can benefit by reading and using many of the ideas and drills shown in the manual.

It's so easy for hitters to fall into bad habits, and these bad habits can be corrected only by repeating the correct hitting mechanics demonstrated. When performing these drills, it is extremely important that each drill be performed correctly because research has shown that it takes seventeen correct muscle movements to correct one wrong movement. Therefore the earlier the correct muscle movement can be programmed into the brain, the easier it will be to become a good hitter.

This manual will fill a void in the basic baseball skill development market. In bookstores and libraries, most baseball books are about present or past professional baseball players. Most are great stories, but few provide the necessary instructions for the development of ball players and managers.

"The Art of Coaching" is a collection of short articles published in a newsletter. Each is designed to help get the most out of each player.

"Bat Selection" explains how to choose the correct bat. It explains why there are different types of bats, gives a method on how to determine the correct weight bat, and states how to deal with wooden bats when reaching pro ball.

"Grip" gives examples of the best method to hold a bat and how much grip pressure should be applied when hitting.

"Plate Coverage" explains why it is so important to get into the same spot in the batter's box every time, as well as how to use the bat as a measuring tool.

"Strike Zone Discipline" explains why the hitter should swing at strikes.

"Ultimate Ingredients for Hitting Success" deals with the recipe of ingredients from desire to visual reminders that are necessary to help develop a good mental approach toward becoming a good hitter.

"Basic Offensive Strategy" emphasizes the need and reasons for a total team effort and the responsibilities needed by each player to score runs and win ball games.

"Basic Hitting Philosophy" deals with the interaction of swing mechanics, concentration, confidence, and strike zone discipline; how they work together; and basic goals every hitter should have.

"Hitting Philosophies and Theories" deals with working on muscle memory and working to be a good hitter.

"Mental Skills for Hitters" explains the importance of the mental side of hitting, taking mental inventory, active awareness, and reframing.

"Running a Good Practice" gives examples of good practice routines, infield and bunting drills, and advanced hitting routine.

"Situation Hitting" gives the offensive strategies for different situations, like what to do with runner held at first, leadoff hitter in the game, runner on third with less than two outs, and more. This chapter is designed to coordinate the offensive strategy of both manager and player.

"Hitting Drills" details forty-five different hitting drills designed to help correct hitting mistakes like stepping into the bucket, casting, and more.

"Becoming a Pro" includes Steve Braun's pinch-hitter deluxe, Doctor Stroke, and the trump card.

"Baseball Statistics" provides basic statistics used to evaluate players and teams.

"The Brothers' Story" is a little about the three authors, Steve, Rich, and Bob.

THE ART OF COACHING

Pencil drawing by Rich Braun

The following is a selection of articles by Bob published in sports newsletters, which are designed to help coaches and players become better. Most of the articles are directed to the development of the next generation, our future. We must all take the time to learn a healthier way, both mentally and physically, in rearing our children and taking control of our lives. Take the time to read the following articles. These articles may point you in the right direction or may simply reinforce what you are already doing.

Art of Coaching 1

Many years ago, when learning the game of baseball, I can remember my father telling my brothers and me that the most important job of a coach is getting the most out of each player. With that philosophy, the success of a coach's ability is not measured by the win-loss record; it's measured by how much improvement each player makes during the season.

This philosophy translates into more than hoping a young player improves. It means spending time with your players at practice and emphasizing that the game is played not just to win but also for fun. It means continually gaining knowledge and improving as a coach. Practice should include drills that keep every player moving and involved. Words of encouragement and praise should be given even if mistakes are made. Always look for the positive and build from there.

If young players feel good about themselves, they are willing to learn. Their play will improve as confidence increases. It's important that confidence be built at an early age, so a coach should always balance playing time and position with ability. Let young players improve and grow before placing them in critical positions like pitcher, catcher, shortstop, or first base. Remember that you are building a person, so be patient, work hard, and always give words of encouragement. Make the game fun for both you and your players.

Art of Coaching 2

The ability to get your message across is vital. If you can't communicate your instructions and ideas to your players, you will not succeed as a coach. When accepting the manager's position of the Kansas City Royals, Bob Boone said, "What a teacher needs is a student. What a student needs is to know that they want to learn about what you know. The key is establishing a relationship."

Getting close to your players and giving them training tools to help you convey your message is the key to coaching success. It is easier if you and the players are on the same page. Use any tool to get your message across. If it's a video, study it yourself and then give it to your players. This will help you both understand what is being taught and what needs to be learned.

Establish a friendship with your players. Make an effort to help them improve both mentally and physically. Always make them feel good about themselves. But you can't let them walk over you, so you must maintain control by making sure everyone knows who's in charge. Enjoy your responsibilities as a coach and continue to make an effort to do your best. You will be rewarded by knowing you are helping your players mature into responsible adults.

Art of Coaching 3

In the past, I've expressed the importance of getting the most out of each player, how a coach should instill confidence, and the idea that the amount of improvement of each player is the measurement of coaching success. The coach's knowledge of baseball and his skill in conveying this knowledge to the players must also be developed.

I've seen great players who were not good coaches, as well as mediocre players who were great coaches. It's important to know baseball, but it's more important to be able to transfer your knowledge. It takes a fine blend of control, confidence, friendship, leadership, and energy.

Kids look up to someone who is in control and has confidence in the knowledge the kids are receiving. Friendship comes by getting to know each player's personality, athletic skills, and weaknesses so that the best method can be used to get your message across. Leadership is obtained by running organized practices where everyone is involved and making the correct decisions during a game. Energy is used by being involved and giving encouragement during the entire practice or game.

Take pride in your leadership role and continue to strive to gather more knowledge about the game through books, clinics, videos, observation of other coaches, or simply playing baseball yourself. Remember, you're not only molding yourself into a caring, concerned person; you're setting an example for tomorrow's future.

Art of Coaching 4

Greatness does not just happen. It takes a fine blend of natural talent, desire to be the best, and what I call coachability. Natural talent plays a big part in determining the eventual level one will obtain, but it's only a part of the formula of greatness. Obviously it helps to be tall, quick, and able to jump to be a great basketball player. Good eye-hand coordination and quick reflexes are necessary to hit a ninety-miles-per-hour fast ball. A finely tuned ear is a must to be a musician. All great individuals have been blessed with some sort of physical natural talent, but many do not reach greatness even though they have talent.

The desire to be the best will propel one beyond what natural talent will do by itself. This desire will stimulate the need to practice and help focus the need. As one improves and receives enjoyment in feeling successful, the need to work harder will be created. As the need to work harder increases, more time (both mentally and physically) will be spent to improve. With more time, the improvement quickens. Soon you have a person who not only understands the importance of listening but also can apply the instructions he or she receives. These people are coachable.

Greatness can be achieved and comes in many forms. It is the responsibility of all coaches, parents, grandparents, teachers, and anyone training our youth to stimulate the desire to be the best they can be. Encouragement, praise, and discipline, and learning to work hard play a big part. Always keep in mind that you are dealing with our future, and the better our children become, the better our future will be.

Art of Coaching 5

Normally, this section is used to provide advice or encouragement to coaches to use positive reinforcement. It is a lot easier if the players know they will receive criticism and praise in a positive manner. In this piece, I would like to touch on another extremely important matter: teaching our children a healthier way.

Today's children are not getting the vitamins and minerals necessary to keep them healthy during their entire lives. With the fast-food restaurants and processed foods, kids are often getting a high-fat diet that does not provide the nutrients to build a strong immune system and help them grow. One out of four children in America are overweight, and most have a very poor diet. It is the responsibility of every adult to educate our youth that eating right should be a way of life. They should know that as athletes, it is important to feed their bodies low-fat foods that are high in fiber and protein and full of vitamins and minerals.

Coaches should instill in them the importance of eating right, and they should include stretching and exercise in every practice. Whether it is running around the bases, sprinting, or having everyone run around the field, some kind of running should be used to build endurance. During practice and games, water should be available.

Make the most out of the time you have your players. In addition to perfecting their athletic skills, teach them to be healthier their entire lives. Remember that athletes use their bodies to perform their sports, and the healthier their bodies, the better our children and the world will be.

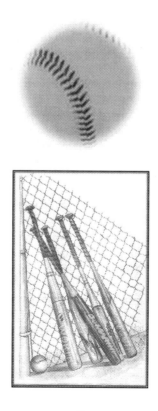

RUNNING A GOOD PRACTICE

It is easier to be prepared for practice if you have developed a good instructional plan. It is important that the players work on less difficult goals in early season practice. As your players master basic skills, you can begin to introduce more advanced skills. One new objective should be established for each practice, with a number of activities and drills used to teach the new skill.

Your practices should be run under a basic format that includes the following.

- Warm-up—warm up the muscles to reduce risk of injuries
- Practice previously taught skills—work on fundamental skills already learned
- Teach and practice new skills—build on players' existing skills
- Practice under game like conditions—stimulate competition
- Cool down—allow athletes' bodies to return to resting state and avoid stiffness
- Evaluate—discuss with your players whether objectives were achieved during practice

All players should have an equal chance to participate and always match players' ability and physical maturity. If you break your team into groups, make sure all groups are matched as equally as possible to prevent one group from always winning. Never put pressure on always winning, but emphasize performing well while giving each player room to make mistakes. Your players will have more fun if they know they will be rewarded if they work hard and are praised when they do well.

Practice Drills

Drills are a great way to review old skills, work on new ones, and even simulate game conditions. The following drills are just a few examples; there are many more. Incorporate them into your practice and always be on the lookout for more. Choose the ones that work on basic skills for earlier practices, then proceed to specialized drills as the first game approaches.

Throwing—To help strengthen throwing muscles and learn throwing accuracy.

Pair up players with each pair having a baseball to throw to each other. Have the catcher give a target with the glove, and have the thrower throw to the glove. Alternate catcher and thrower with each throw. To create competition, give the thrower one point if the ball would have hit the catcher's body and two points for the head. The first to score twenty-one points wins.

Coaching Points—Encourage the thrower to concentrate at throwing to the glove. Make sure the throwers are throwing over the top, not sidearm.

Grounders—To practice the fundamentals of fielding ground balls and quick ball release.

Break players into two lines. Position one line at the shortstop position and the other line at second base position. Have a player start at first base. Hit a ground ball to the first in line at shortstop. After the player at shortstop catches the grounder and throws to first, he rotates to the end of the line at second base. The player at second base moves to first base after making the play. The player at first base rotates to the end of the line at shortstop after catching throws from both lines. Increase the speed of the game as fielding improves.

Coaching Points—Make sure each player is fielding the grounder correctly and using two hands for quick ball release. This drill is good for working on previously taught skills.

BATTING PRACTICE ROUTINE

Batting practice routine should be used to simulate, as much as possible, game situations. This can involve both the hitter and fielders. It is easy for young and even older players to lose focus if not involved or active. Baseball is a game where the action can sometimes be slow. It is important to develop a well-organized practice where players are not simply standing around. The following batting practice routines are designed to help coaches work on individual problems, develop strike zone discipline, stimulate competition, and teach team unity while keeping all players focused.

There are many ways to set up a batting practice routine, but try to develop an easy routine at the beginning and then progress to more complex routines as the players improve and mature. One thing that can be guaranteed with a controlled, organized, and well-run routine is that each player can and will improve.

Control must be established at the first practice. Never let the players start the practice with hitting without an order how batters will hit. Batting order is a way to establish hitting order. Another is the order the players arrive at practice. This is good because it encourages players to get to practice early or on time.

A good way to warm up hitting muscles is to have the on-deck hitter hit off a tee into the backstop. By starting off with the tee, coaches have a perfect opportunity to use the drills in this manual to work on individual problems.

Never go into hitting practice without a set routine on how many swings each batter takes. Any more then fifteen swings at one time is too many. It is better to go five to ten swings two or three times instead of allowing the hitter to continue to hit over and over. This is how bad habits are formed.

Each hitter should bunt the first three to five pitches so that he or she can learn to bunt. This also helps the batter follow the ball to the bat and get used to the speed of the pitch. The bunts should be toward the first or third base line.

Drill: A good way to work on bunting and stimulate competition is to have all the players line up at home plate to bunt. The object is to be the last player in the game. To continue to play, the ball must be bunted fair. If foul, the batter is out of the game. Losers must run a lap around the bases.

Coaching Points—Check to make sure all the hitters are bunting correctly. If any are having a problem, take them aside to work with them. Do this drill only two or three times. It moves pretty quickly and is fun for the kids.

Another good way to promote competition is to set up two- or three-man hitting teams. Try to match each team as equally as possible so that each has a chance to win. Fielders are set up in normal fielding positions. The object for the hitters is to get base hits. The object of the fielders is to get three outs.

Each hitter steps into the box as if it is a game. Balls and strikes are called, but no walks are allowed because this is hitting practice. Errors are not counted as hits and the fielders must throw out the runners or catch fly balls to make outs, just like a game. Because hits are counted and there is a winner and loser, all players stay focused and work hard to get hits or make outs. It is as close to game conditions as possible without playing a game. It is important that the manager or coach maintain control of calling balls and strikes and determining errors and hits by controlling calls. Discipline and control must be established. A team that has managers and coaches in control has a better chance of improving and winning games.

Notes

ADVANCED BATTING PRACTICE ROUTINE

The main goals of this section are as follows.

1. To develop practice habits that allow hitters to take advantage of their abilities.
2. To perfect the skills necessary to produce a line drive swing with maximum bat speed and aggressiveness.
3. For hitters to perfect the skills of situation hitting.

First Round

Two sacrifice bunts
One squeeze bunt
One fake bunt and Slash

Four situation swings: A, B, C, D (determined each day)

A. Hit and run
B. Move runner from second to third, no outs
C. Get runner in from third, infield back
D. Get runner in from third, infield in

Four Swings: The hitter's mindset is being above the ball and on top. His or her mindset is to hit the ball toward the opposite side of the mound on the ground.
One bunt for a base hit (run to first base and become a runner.)

Second Round

Four swings: The hitter's mindset is to hit the ball on a line to the gaps. Aggressiveness and bat speed are increased.

Third Round

Number of swings is determined by the manager, and swings are used to make adjustments from earlier rounds.

All pregame practice is for the purpose of hitting line drives. Hitters are not attempting to lift the ball over the fence. Poor batting practice creates bad habits, which consequently result in poor game performance. All work on mechanics and individual instruction should be done during extra batting practice.

SITUATION HITTING

Proper Execution in Situations Results for Winning Baseball

Know the situation you are in and what you have to do to advance base runners. Know the pitcher and what he or she will probably do to try to get an out. Use batting practice routine to practice execution of situation hitting.

The following are hitting situations that are important to the team in building a consistent scoring attack. These situations are flexible according to the manager's philosophy. The manager will let the hitter know what his or her role is when it comes to situation hitting. Not every hitter will be asked to carry out every one of the following situations. Every hitter should know the purpose of situation hitting and how it fits into the manager's offensive strategy.

1. Leadoff hitter in the Game

The hitter should take a strike if the count goes to 2–0. Some starting pitchers struggle early in the game with their control. Getting the starter in trouble early is important, so make the starter prove he or she can throw strikes.

2. Hitter Leading Off an Inning When a New Pitcher Enters

The hitter takes 2–0 late in the game depending on the game situation and manager's preference. The exception here is if the hitter can zone for his or her pitch. By zoning, your chances for the extra-base hit that would put the winning run in scoring position are greater. A relief pitcher can struggle when he or she enters the game. Make sure the pitcher can throw strikes, and always let the pitcher beat himself or herself.

3. Runner Held at First

Left-Handed Hitter—When the runner is held at first early in the count, the hitter should look to pull the ball in the hole between first and second.

Right-Handed Hitter—When the runner is held at first, the hitter should look for a ball to drive in the hole between first and second.

Runner Stealing Base—The hitter should zone for the pitch and swing if it is in his or her personal hitting zone, but the hitter should take if it is not. The exception here is if the game is close late in the game. The hitter may want to take to allow the base stealer to get into scoring position.

Hitting to the hole between first and second is an important skill to execute for a few reasons. First, if the batter hits the ball in the hole to right field, the runner on first can advance more than one base. Each ninety feet is one-fourth of a run, and the closer the runner is to home plate, the easier it is to produce a full run. Also, the team is only going to get so many hits in each game, so the hitter must move each runner as many bases as possible with each hit. Second, by attempting to hit the hole, it is easier to stay out of the double play when the ball is hit to the right side. Third, if a fast runner is on first and the hitter doesn't succeed in hitting the ball through the hole, he forces the second baseman to go to first. Looking for and reacting to the right pitch, plus moving up or back from the plate, is key to executing the skills mentioned, such as hitting on the right side.

4. Runner on Second, No Outs, Early in the Game

Left-Handed Hitter—Should attempt to drive the runner in by pulling the ball to right field. The hitter may move closer to the plate to get a pitch to pull.

Right-Handed Hitter—Should attempt to drive the run in by hitting ball to the right side. The hitter may move off the plate in order for the ball to be out over the plate.

Early in the game, the hitter is not giving himself or herself up. At this point in the game, you are looking for the big inning, and you do not want to give up outs. In the attempt to drive the ball to the right side, if the hitter does not get a hit, the runner still moves up to third base.

Two exceptions would be if the hitter is not swinging the bat well, or you are facing a pitcher with which you have had trouble. In both cases, the hitter may want to give himself or herself up to move the runner.

5. Runner on Second with No Outs, Late in the Game, Score Close

Left-Handed Hitter—Must make contact and pull the ball to the right side.

Right-handed Hitter—Must make contact and hit the ball to the right side.

In both cases, the hitter's mindset should be "Keep the ball out of the air and get the runner to third." The hitter may choke up on the bat for more control, and he or she should always choke up with two strikes. Here, you are playing for the run to win the game and are willing to give up an out to get that run.

6. Runner on Third, Less Than Two Outs, Infield In

The hitter's mindset is to drive the ball on a line to the center fielder, but it does not mean he or she must hit it there. This mindset helps him or her stay on the ball.

The hitter must keep the ball away from the corners. Some pitchers will throw a changeup or curve in this situation, hoping for the ground ball to the corners. The hitter should not try to lift the ball in this situation; his or her mindset is a line drive stroke.

7. Runner on Third, Less Than Two Outs, Infield Back

The hitter's mindset is to drive the ball to center fielder until he or she has one strike. After the hitter has one strike, the hitter chokes up, shortens his or her swing, gets on top of the pitch, and hits the ball up the middle, away from the corners.

8. Hit and Run

Runner at first breaks, and the hitter protects the runner. The hitter's number one job is to make contact, and his or her number two responsibility is to hit the ball on the ground. He or she should hit the ball where it is pitched, because hitting to the vacated hole can be difficult on certain pitches. Think, and stay on top of the ball.

Bunting Situations

Runner on First Base—Make the first baseman field the bunt.

Runners on First and Second—Make the worst fielder (first or third baseman) field the bunt. It is safer to kill the ball toward first base than it is to try to bunt it past the pitcher to the third baseman. The exception is if the first baseman is an excellent fielder who can throw the runner out at third base.

Make the pitcher throw a strike. A walk is better than a sacrifice bunt. Also, if the hitter can get an advantage in the count, the manager may change strategy by letting the hitter hit away. The hitter should know when the situation calls for a drag bunt or push ball for a hit. If the hitter becomes a good bunter, the manager may give him or her the sign to bunt for a hit.

9. Bunting for a Base Hit

This is a weapon that all hitters should be able to use, especially faster runners. The reputation of being able to bunt for a hit will bring the infielders in and create more holes for ground ball hits. Practicing bunting techniques will give you confidence to bunt for a hit and not feel it is a wasted at bat. Know when the situation is good to bunt. The following are not good situations to try to bunt for a hit.

    a. Two outs, no one on, and the hitter is not a base stealer, or he or she has the ability to hit a double.

    b. Two outs, runner on second base. A bunt won't score the run.

    c. Ahead by a lot of runs.

    d. Late in the game, and the hitter has extra-base power.

10. Fake Bunt and Slash

Whenever the sacrifice bunt is on, in a first and second situation, the hitter has the option to fake a bunt and slash if the infielders are moving in. Watch for the wheel play by the opposing manager in the first and second situation late in the game.

Proper execution of the slash is to turn to bunt with weight on the hitter's back foot. The bat is pulled back, and the ball is slapped on the ground past the charging infielders.

OFF-SEASON TRAINING

Off-season is the time to work on increasing strength and endurance and to develop mental capabilities. It's a perfect time to work on basic skills, concentration, and develop good work habits. It is a time to work on weaknesses and allow injuries to heal.

Training should include weight training for the major muscle groups, sprints for quickness, and long-distance running for cardiovascular development. For the young athlete, light weight with high reps is recommended for a maximum of two sets. The weight training should be done at least twice a week. Endurance training should be performed three times a week. This could include running, cross-country skiing, cycling, or anything to make the heart work harder for at least twenty minutes.

Remember that any additional strength will improve performance. Also, do not expect the youngster to automatically develop good work habits. It is up to the parent, coach, grandparent, or friend to find time and a positive way to encourage the development of an off-season training program. Make the off-season training fun, and take the time to make training a way of life. Both you and the ball player will become better friends.

Off-season training should also include hitting off the tee. This allows the hitter to work on the fundamentals of the swing while strengthening the hitting muscles. This can be done in a cellar, a garage, or anywhere you can hang a hitting screen, net, or blanket. This also can be done inside when it is too cold outside. The hitter should swing a heavier bat to warm up and cool down. This will help strengthen the hitting muscles.

Notes

BASEBALL STATISTICS

Baseball statistics play an important role in evaluating the progress of a player and team. They provide managers and players a record of how they are doing and improving over the course of the baseball season. Statistics are used to measure batting, baserunning, pitching, and fielding, as well as overall player value. There are a ton of statistics that are available. We'll just give the basic ones here.

Batting—The measurement to evaluate a hitter's success as a hitter.

There are a number of statistics to measure a hitter's success, but the basic core is batting average, RBI, and home runs.

a. Batting average (BA): Divide the number of hits by the number of at bats. 5 for 10 = .500.

b. Run batted in (RBI): The number of runners scored by hitter's by getting a base hit, sacrifice fly, walk, and any other way, except hitting into a double play or reach by an error.

c. Home run (HR): The number of times a hitter touches all four bases in an at-bat without a fielding error.

Baserunning—The measurement of a runner's ability to steal a base.

a. Stolen base (SB): The number of bases a runner steals when the defense has the ball.

b. Caught stealing (CS): The number of times caught stealing when trying to steal a base.

c. Stolen base attempts (SBA or ATT): Number of times a player attempted to steal a base.

d. Stolen base percentage (SB%): The percent of successful steals. Stolen bases divided by attempts.

Pitching—The measurement of success a pitcher is pitching.

a. Base on balls (BB): The four balls to hitter that put hitter on first base.

b. Number of batters faced (BF): Plate appearances of other team faced by pitcher in a game.

c. Earn run average (ERA): The number of earned runs multiplied by 9, then divided by total innings pitched. Example: 5 earn runs, 20 innings pitched. $5 \times 9 = 45 / 20 = 2.25$ ERA.

d. Losses (L): The number of games where the opposing team took the lead while the pitcher was pitching, and the opposing team went on to win the game.

e. Wins (W): The number of games the pitcher's team took a lead while he or she was pitching, and the team went on to win.

There are many more baseball statistics that are available to measure all parts of the game. If you are interested in finding more of the statistics, you can find them in *The Complete Encyclopedia of Baseball* by Hy Turkin (published in 1951), *Baseball Encyclopedia*, and *Total Baseball*.

BAT SELECTION

Because physical characteristics differ from player to player, there are many different models of bats. It is important to find a bat that is comfortable and fits the hitting style being used. At one time, almost all hitters used heavy bats. Today, hitters have a great variety from which to choose. Experiment and choose a bat most comfortable for you.

One thing to keep in mind while choosing a bat is hand size. If the hands are small, you should not get a bat with a thick handle. Gripping a bat properly with small hands and a thick handle can be a problem.

But speed and quickness are important, especially in the rotation hitting style, where the focus is on the hips and core as the primary source of power. The point of rotational hitting is to swing the bat with the entire body. If you use this hitting style, you may consider using a light bat with a thin handle. This type gives you greater quickness and bat speed. It can give you a feeling of whipping the bat with your hands, not your body. If the bat is too heavy, you can lose the whipping feel, but be careful about using one that is too light. If it is too light, the ball will not jump off the bat with as much velocity. Find a happy medium.

Players using the weight shift hitting style may choose to go to a little heavier bat. The weight shifting style is where one takes the weight off the front foot, shifts it to the back foot, and then retransfers the weight back to the front foot during the swing. In using this style, the hitter is using less snapping or whipping of the hands and more of a pulling action of the lead arm.

Any size bat or model will work with any hitting style, but there are some common factors that make sense. The most important thing when choosing a bat is that the bat feels comfortable. A good way to determine the proper weight is by holding the bat with the left hand if hitting from the right side, or your right hand if hitting left-handed, with the pinkie hanging over the end of the bat. With the bat at your side and elbow straight, raise the bat. If the elbow must be bent to raise the bat, then the bat is too heavy.

Most hitters haven't been exposed to a large variety of wood bat models. A good time to experiment is when you first get into pro ball. There are usually lots of different models around most clubhouses. Also, when experimenting with these new bats, seek the advice of one of the hitting instructors; they have seen many models over their careers and can be very helpful in this area.

Another thing to remember when using a wooden bat (this is not a factor when using the aluminum bat) is the label is either held up facing the hitter or down facing the ground. This lines up the grain of the bat properly. If it is held with the label facing the pitcher or facing the catcher, it isn't as strong and will break easily.

GRIP

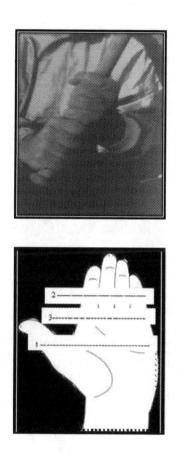

Your grip should be firm but also relaxed and comfortable. There are three basic ways the bat can be held. One of the three ways gives the hitter an advantage. The three ways are (1) deep in the palm or choked, (2) higher up in the fingers, and (3) where the fingers meet the palms. There are disadvantages in grips 1 and 2, and the most advantage is in grip 3. The disadvantage to grip 1 is it puts the bat so far back in the palm that the fingertips do not provide enough contact with the bat. The greater sense of feel of grip 3 gives the hitter greater control of the bat.

It is similar to the surgeon who holds the scalpel: he or she holds it in the fingertips. This gives him or her a greater sense of feel and control, and the instrument can be maneuvered precisely. Would you have surgery done by a surgeon who choked his or her scalpel?

Grip 2 puts the bat more in the fingers. Holding the bat this way takes the bat almost completely out of the palm, which is the strongest part of the hand.

When the hitter puts the bat only in the fingers, he or she loses stability and control. Holding the bat where the thumb pad meets the palm gives the bat stability. At the point of contact, the hitter is redirecting great force created by the mass of the thrown ball. If the bat isn't stable, the bat can almost be knocked out of the hitter's hands.

The most desirable grip is grip 3. This grip allows the fingertips to have enough contact with the bat. It also gives enough stability because the bat has contact where the thumb pad meets the palm.

Again, it's important to experiment with different handle thicknesses. Put the handle in the areas described and feel the difference in each grip. Think about the advantages and disadvantages.

Another important point to remember is that hitters who use the choking grip (grip 1) sometimes also wrap the top hand all the way around the bat with the knuckles facing the pitcher. This hand position puts the thumb pad of the top hand under the bat instead of behind it at contact. This is a very weak position. Putting the hand behind the bat helps absorb the shock of the pitched ball. Also, holding the bat this way can limit top hand extension, because the wrist is cocked inwardly instead of outwardly. This inward hand position will cause the bat to start up and out of the strike zone too soon, rather than staying down and through.

Also important is how much grip pressure you apply to the handle. The hitter has an advantage if he chooses the middle ground—not too tight but not too loose. Holding the bat too tight causes the forearms to tighten. This restricts the hand action, which causes the swing to be slower. This especially affects the quickness needed for the rotation hitting style.

Holding the bat too loosely can cause the hitter to lose a sense of aggressiveness. Also, he or she can lose bat stability. Strive for a grip that is in between the two extremes.

Another grip that has become popular is putting the little finger of the bottom hand over the knob. This grip is strongly discouraged because of the large number of injuries to a small bone in the hand.

Notes

_____

_____

_____

_____

_____

_____

_____

_____

_____

_____

_____

PLATE COVERAGE

Plate coverage is an area of hitting that is extremely important but is overlooked by many hitters. The main goal in having plate coverage is to find the proper place in the batter's box for your hitting style and approach to the ball.

If the weight shift style is used, the general rule is deeper in the box and off the plate. Hitters using the rotation style generally should be at midpoint in the box and closer to the plate. Slight adjustments are OK because the way hitters approach the ball varies. Standing in the places described gives the barrel a chance to move consistently through the strike zone during the swing. Getting too far from the positions described goes against the principles of the two hitting styles. The weight shift style hitters who stand too close to the plate will get jammed if they stride properly. Rotation hitters who stand too far off the plate can lose plate coverage because of the outward rotation of their swing. The hit style hitters use and how they approach the ball will be the deciding factor in where they stand in the box.

You are encouraged to experiment so you can find the right place in the box. After finding the right place, find a way to get there every time. Consistency is extremely important. If the hitter is not consistent, he or she will lack outside coverage one time and then too much coverage the next.

One way to be consistent is using the bat as a measuring tool. You should step into a batter's box and place your feet where you think they should be. After taking your normal stride and swing, look at the barrel as it passes over the plate. Adjust the feet until you can see the barrel covering the plate. Once you have your feet where you want them, touch a corner of the plate with the bat. This touch system assures you are in the same place each time you enter the box.

There may be times when the hitter should move closer or farther from the plate. Game situations sometimes will dictate where the hitter stands. There will be times when the hitter would help the team by either pushing or pulling the ball. Don't be reluctant to make adjustments in the box that will help you carry out offensive strategy. (See the chapter on offensive strategy.)

STRIKE ZONE DISCIPLINE

Ted Williams said it best: "My first rule of hitting was to get a good ball to hit."

It's very simple. Except for a very few gifted hitters, most people find it much easier to hit if they hit strikes. I'm sure you have heard a pitching coach yell to his pitcher, "Get ahead of the hitters." That tells you it must be easier for him or her to pitch when he's ahead. You must remember if you swing at pitches three inches off the borders of the plate, you have increased the strike zone over 30 percent. By swinging at pitches in this area, you will consistently hit behind in the count, which is not to your advantage.

There are exceptions, but most of the great hitters in the game today are selective at the plate and work pitchers into favorable counts. The question is, How did they learn to select pitches? The most important thing is knowing the importance of discipline at the plate. If you don't share this philosophy and its importance, you will never make an effort to work on the skills needed to judge balls and strikes.

Reading a pitch and making the decision to swing or not is a skill most hitters can learn through repetition. The hitters must make a conscious effort to make sure they are swinging at strikes in hitting practice. Also, a certain amount of batting practice must be at game speed. You can do this by having the batting practice pitcher throw from a shorter distance. This cuts down the read time on the pitch, making it appear to be at game like speed. From the shorter distance, read the pitch and make the decision on whether or not to swing. By practicing this way, the hitter's quick judgment skills will improve greatly.

Hitting strikes is especially important with runners in scoring position. In these situations, the pitcher wants you to hit his pitch. Thus, he will miss more often, so the hitter must be patient and not get overanxious. This is extremely important if you expect to knock in the big runs.

The following 1981 study proves the advantages of hitting ahead in the count. The following figures were compiled after 52 games and 1,741 at bats. They reflect the batting averages compiled with various counts.

| 0–0: .318 | 1–0: .359 | 2–0: .373 | 3–0: .250 | 1–1: .282 | 2–1: .366 |
| 3–1: .365 | 3–2: .263 | 0–1: .194 | 0–2: .094 | 1–2: .166 | 2–2: .263 |

Notice in every count except 3–0, the hitter had a higher average when he was ahead in the count. Now you know why the pitching coach yells to his pitcher to pitch ahead! The game between the pitcher and hitter is a game within itself, and the hitter can't beat himself if he's going to win that game. Ask pitchers whom they like to pitch to, and most of them will say the wild swinger.

We don't want a team full of nonaggressive hitters, but we do want hitters to understand the advantages of strike zone discipline. The thing to strive for is controlled aggression.

ULTIMATE INGREDIENTS FOR HITTING SUCCESS

1. **Desire**—To wish, long for, or crave something. *Crave* means "to yearn for or desire intensely."

You must be obsessed with your desire to hit. Hitting is a difficult skill to master. There are no shortcuts, no easy ways out. There will be many bumps in the road and many tough moments. There will be series of bad at bats, bad games, bad weeks, and maybe even bad months. There may be thoughts of quitting or "I can't hit." But if you start with a strong desire and have the physical ability, you'll overcome any obstacle in your way. Every great Major League hitter has a burning desire to be the best he can, and he won't let anything stand in his way.

2. **Patience**—The capability of bearing delay.

Every hitter wants positive results immediately. That's understandable, but that's not the way learning to hit works. Your journey is much like that of the baby learning to walk. The child first tries to get up then falls. The child will get up, maybe take some steps, and then fall again; this process continues until he or she walks. Hitting is the same way. You'll have a bad day and then make some adjustments and have some good days. Then you'll have some more bad days. The important thing is that you fully understand this is a process, and there is no getting around it. The sooner you understand that this is a process that is unavoidable, the sooner you can stop beating up on yourself when you're struggling.

You have to realize that moving yourself from a sometimes awkward young player into a pro prospect doesn't come overnight. It takes day after day, month after month, and season after season of perseverance and patience. Concentrate on small steps, cementing them firmly into place one brick at a time. Soon you'll have a strong foundation on which to build.

3. **Faith**—Believing in something that cannot be seen, heard, or proven.

You must believe that through hard, smart work, you'll be rewarded with success. You must believe that if you keep a positive attitude and learn something every day, you'll have a payoff. There will be times when you have no proof that you will succeed. You will have to believe. There will be times when you will lose faith in yourself. You must always go back and get it. Without faith, you're going nowhere. Good things will always happen if you have faith. That's how important faith is.

4. **Dedication**—To be devoted to a special purpose.

You must want to become a better hitter and be dedicated to that purpose. You must set goals and let nothing stand in your way of reaching those goals. There will be lots of things trying to stop you—negative and jealous people, drugs, laziness, curve balls, night life, and bad days. But you must take a tough stand for what you want and not let anything get in your way. You should write the following statement down and read it every day.

"I will never stop working to get better, no matter how hard the struggle may be. I will persevere despite the hard times I have ahead of me."

5. **Confidence**—The thought of believing in something that has not already happened. The feeling of assurance or certainty.

This is the toughest ingredient to acquire and keep. Confidence comes and goes. The people who stay confident for longer periods have a positive, lighthearted outlook. They have good attitudes and believe good things will happen. They forget bad days and never carry the negative past with them. They're always replacing a negative with a positive. It may be dinner, positive conversation with a special person, or a call home. Forgetting failures is the first step to regaining lost confidence. You can accomplish that by getting your mind on something else. It's also important to understand that if you have patience, faith, and dedication, confidence will come. The word *confidence* is a key that you'll need no matter what you do in life. It comes from two Latin words, *con* meaning with, and *fideo* meaning faith. "With faith" is confidence. Without faith, there is zero confidence.

6. Final Conscious Pre-swing Thought

Before discussing what final conscious thought is, let's explain the difference between the conscious mind and the subconscious mind. The brain acts much like a computer in that it stores the information you put into it. The conscious or slow-thinking mind is your inner voice. It's the voice with which you talk to yourself. The subconscious mind is the mind that allows you to react to a pitch and tells you how to swing.

The final pre-swing thought is the last thing you hear from your inner voice. It's your last thought before you react to the pitch. You can control this thought, so why not think positively? If your final thought is "home run," you're dead—it will cause you to tighten up and pull off the ball. If your mind is racing with negative thoughts, your subconscious mind has difficulty taking over and performing the swing.

Your last conscious thought should be something individual because each hitter has different tendencies and different swing problems. If you have tight hands or shoulders your final thought might be, "Soft hands and let it happen," or perhaps "Relax and feel the sweet spot." Whatever that thought is, trust it and make it a routine. It clears and relaxes the mind and allows the body to react naturally to the ball. At what time to use it is also an individual thing. As a general rule, it is used just prior to when the pitcher releases the ball.

7. Visual Reminders

Hitting is said to be the single most difficult thing to do in sports. It will test your mind, body, and character. There will be good days and bad days. Even the best will fail seven out of ten times. To be an effective hitter takes a lot of preparation. You also must learn to be your own coach. It takes learning what you have to do to be a consistent hitter. Preparing to hit is reminding yourself of basic principles and fundamentals.

Every hitter should compile a list of words or short phrases that will help clear the mind. Again, this list should be individualized so you can key your swing movement. This will help clear the mind of negative thoughts.

Here are some examples of visual reminders: relaxation, rhythm and balance, stride slow and easy, keep hands back as I stride, head still, see the ball hit the bat, upper body stacked, level body parts, level swing plane, drive through the ball, quick hands, and five hitting phases. Your list should contain words or phrases that cure your hitting problems. Before you compile your list, you have to analyze your hitting problems. You have to ask yourself, "What do I do wrong when I'm not swinging the bat well?" These words or phrases should be written down on a piece of paper and looked at when needed. You'll be surprised at how it can explain a bad day at the plate and give you something to work on the next day.

8. The Level Cut (Line Drive) Swing

Kids start playing organized tee ball at age five or six years old and normally use bats too heavy for their underdeveloped arms and hands. Therefore, they drop their back shoulders and swing with their big muscles in a long, sweeping action. This drops the bat barrel behind the body in a long arc and causes the hitter to lift the ball off the tee rather than drive through the ball. Another thing that programs the long uppercut is the thrill of the touchdown pass, the slam dunk, and the home run. We see them every night on SportsCenter, with Aaron Judge, Mike Trout, Bryce Harper, and all the rest hitting four-hundred-foot home runs. The hard ground ball, line drive swing is what you should strive for. Why? Because 90 percent of fly balls are unproductive, whereas only 60 percent of ground balls are unproductive. A team that hits twenty-seven-line drives or ground balls will score a few runs by the seventh inning, whereas a team that hits twenty-seven fly balls will have a difficult time scoring runs.

Notes

BASIC HITTING PHILOSOPHY

Swing mechanics—Mastery of the basic swing mechanics.

Concentration—The ability to become absorbed in the action of hitting.

Confidence—The deep belief you can hit any pitcher.

Strike zone discipline—The ability to judge balls and strikes.

Swing Mechanics

Concentration

Strike Zone Discipline

Confidence

Each one of these four things feed off each other, making the others possible. It starts with the basic mechanics of the swing. If you have mastered them, you will get base hits. If you get base hits, your confidence level will increase. With a high level of confidence, you will be able to relax and concentrate. With a high level of concentration, you will see the ball better, enabling you to judge balls and strikes. As you can see, you can't have one without the other, and without all four, it is difficult to become a complete hitter.

There are three basic goals every hitter should have whenever he or she picks up a baseball bat.

1. Direction—Learn to control the bat so you can control the ball. In batting practice, learn to hit holes and the gaps.
2. Height—Hit the ball at the proper height, which is on the line.
3. Velocity—Hit the ball hard so it will find the holes and the gaps.

BASIC OFFENSIVE STRATEGY

To understand the offensive part of baseball, one must realize that the offensive part is no different than any other team sport. That is, each hitter has his or her responsibility according to the play being run, the situation of the game, and the count the hitter is hitting in during the inning.

With the running back in football, his responsibilities change from play to play according to the situation of the game. Because hitting is an individual skill, one sometimes forgets about offensive strategy and situational hitting.

What you will read on the following pages is nothing complicated. They are basic things every player must know and understand before the team can succeed. The objective in this section is to get hitters to realize the importance of executing basic offensive strategy. If you don't know the importance of offensive strategy, you won't work on the skills needed to make that strategy work.

Every player must know there is more to hitting than just swinging the bat. Players should realize they are given the chance to execute offensive strategy by the manager, for the good of the team.

Every hitter on the team is part of an offensive unit. That unit is nine hitters against one pitcher. Think about that. How can one pitcher beat nine hitters if they are working together? The following are three basic goals every team should have.

1. Getting runners on base (preferably the leadoff hitter)
2. Advancing the runner or runners
3. Scoring the runner or runners

Every player must realize if the team is going to be successful offensively, each hitter has a role or job. Players also must realize that their job changes with each at bat, according to the situation of the game.

Before the start of the inning, hitters must know what the team needs to win the game and how their jobs will change as the inning progresses. It's the hitter's responsibility at the start of an inning to know the following.

1. The score of the game
2. What inning it is
3. How many outs there are as the inning progresses

Going over these things in their minds beforehand will make it easier for hitters to respond to the manager's strategy as the inning unfolds. Also, if you know the manager's strategy ahead of time, it will be easier to perform the skills needed to execute the strategy. Don't ever be caught by surprise. Being surprised is being unprepared, and failure is a by-product of not being prepared.

HITTING PHILOSOPHIES AND THEORIES

Because players vary in physical characteristics, hitting style must also vary. There are two basic hitting styles. Identify what style is suited for you and then perfect the fundamentals of that style.

Every hitter must develop a hitting style to take advantage of his or her physical characteristics. A player's physical characteristics, running speed, strength, hand quickness, physical size, and eye-hand coordination vary. It is important for both players and coaches to understand this principle. No two players are alike; they differ in body types, bone length, and muscle structure. But they do fit into certain categories. Some have great speed, and others have average speed. Some have great strength, whereas some have average strength. Some have great bat quickness, and others have average bat quickness. All hitters are not created equal, so you can't make them into something they can't become. Once this principle is understood, each player can fit into one of the basic hitting styles. Only then can a player reach his or her full offensive potential.

For example, not all hitters can hold their hands close to their bodies, bat vertical, use the top hand, and be quick like Ted Williams. But a hitter may be able to hold the hands back, flatten the bat, pull with the bottom hand, and shift his or her weight like George Brett.

It's important to remember each movement must be consciously thought about and practiced in order to make it part of your muscle memory. Muscle memory is identical to mind memory. Read a paragraph five times, and you won't have it memorized. Read it five more times, and you'll remember a few phrases and maybe a few sentences. Read it one hundred times aloud, and you will have it memorized. Muscle memory works the same way. Correctly perform the movements of hitting over and over, and you can't help but develop a sound swing. If you are practicing the movements incorrectly, you will put the incorrect movements into you muscle memory. Therefore, it is always important to have a coach monitor your progress.

Many people say great hitters are born, not made. This is not true. Don't misunderstand this statement; there were many great natural born hitters. Rod Carew, Tony Oliva, Ted Williams, Stan Musial, Al Kaline, Derek Jeter, and Ty Cobb, to name a few, were all natural hitters. But for every natural hitter, there are five who made themselves great hitters by having good work habits, such as George Brett, Pete Rose, Carl Yastrzemski, Wade Boggs, Hal McRae, Lou Piniella, Dewy Evans, Kirby Puckett, Matt Williams, and one of the best examples, Mike Schmidt. Each of these guys had to work extra hard to perfect his hitting style. But more important, these hitters had to work smart to reach the level they did. They had to get in the batting cage and use their heads to make themselves great. Remember, great athletes learn their skills and then compete with their minds. The smarter person will ultimately win the day.

MENTAL SKILLS FOR HITTERS

The mental side of hitting is very critical. Having a positive mental attitude every game, every at bat, and every pitch over the long baseball season is the most important asset a hitter can possess. Without it, the hitter can't concentrate and control his or her nervous system to allow the hitting skills to work.

The difference between a .270 hitter and a .310 hitter each with 500 at bats (ABs) is one hit a week over the twenty-week minor league season. That means only one hit a week separates the average hitter from the best hitters. How many ABs have you given away because you were not mentally ready to hit? How many because of lack of intensity, lack of concentration, lack of determination, thinking of past performances, self-doubt, pressing and trying too hard, not relaxing, thinking too much, or being negative? These mental distractions make hitters do the things they do at the plate. They cause the mechanical problems. Change the way you think, and you can change the way you hit.

The confrontation between the pitcher and hitter is a game within a game. It's very challenging and will test your character. This game is won or lost by what goes on between your ears. It is just as important to learn mental skills as it is to learn the physical skills of hitting. There have been hitters with good mechanics but a bad mental attitude who didn't hit.

The biggest obstacle a hitter has is a negative mindset. Your mind sometimes can be your biggest handicap. It can also be your biggest asset. Being a successful hitter depends more on strength of mind than strength of body. When you start to understand what goes on inside of you, you'll be able to manage yourself and your attitude.

Important Points

1. The difference between a .270 hitter and a .310 hitter is one hit a week. Learn why you did or didn't get that hit! If you didn't make it, it may be your attitude.
2. The game between the pitcher and hitter is won or lost by what goes on between your ears.
3. Your mind can be your greatest handicap or your greatest asset.

There are mental skills you can learn so you can manage your mental state. These skills are important because they allow you to have a consistent, more positive frame of mind. They also will help control the nervous system so you can relax. When you're relaxed and focused, your hitting skills are free to react to the pitch.

Learning to deal with all the distractions and mind games is essential if you are going to reach your full potential. The high-performance state of mind leads to a high concentration level, composure under pressure, clear vision, and mental strategy that leads to peak performance. This is the mindset of all great athletes. This separates great hitters from average hitters. The great hitters train their minds just as hard as they train their swing mechanics. Great hitters develop mental fitness.

When you develop and use mental fitness skills, you create a state of relaxed concentration. You are relaxed physically, in control of your thinking, feeling positive, confident, and you have a sense of just letting it happen at the plate.

Most athletes have no training in mental skills and therefore they don't know the importance of learning those skills. It is important to understand it's no different than learning any skill.

How many times have you heard the hitter say, "I'm not seeing the ball," or, "I don't feel good at the plate"? Not being able to see the ball or not feeling good are mental problems, which in turn become physical problems. When you go to the plate with self-doubt, your nervous system gets out of whack. This causes muscle tension, which "pinches" nerve impulses. This results in the tightening of the muscles in your eyes, hands, and legs. This is why you don't see the ball or feel good. You are tight, anxious, and jumpy instead of relaxed and smooth.

Important Points

1. Mental fitness leads to a peak performance state of mind. This leads to high levels of concentration, clear vision, composure under pressure, and mental strategy.
2. Great athletes train their minds just as hard as their bodies.
3. Self-doubt causes muscle tension, which leads to bad vision and tight hands and legs.

Learning mental skills to help stay in a positive mental state starts with taking mental inventory. You must be aware of what you're feeling mentally when you are going well and what you're feeling mentally when you are going bad. Your mental state will change from day to day, and you must be aware of where you are at the present time. Once you are aware, you can change and control how you think and feel. If you can mentally review each pitch to you and remember how you felt, you're on the way to developing mental fitness.

Only after sensing what's going on inside of you as a result of several bad at bats can you begin to do something about how you feel. Until you can control the way you think and feel, you will be fighting an uphill battle.

It starts with sensing how you feel and what you're thinking in certain situations during the game. You must be honest as you ask yourself, "How did I really feel? What was I thinking before, during, and after each at bat? Was I a little nervous? If I was, did my hands tighten up? Was I really focused and feeling confident? Was I intense and determined to succeed? Was I intimidated in any way? Did I really want to be up with the game on the line?" How you think and feel during an at bat will have a direct effect on your pitch selection and how you swing the bat. This is taking mental inventory.

You can't separate how you are thinking and feeling from how your body is working. The mind and body are directly connected. Professional hitters understand their minds can get out of focus, and they know what to do about it. They simply talk themselves back to where they want their minds to be. They feed the mind positive self-talk if they need it. They don't allow negative thought processes to occupy their minds and clear them out before entering the batter's box. This is why professional hitters appear relaxed and confident at the plate. They can sense when their minds are wandering or if they feel tight. But more important, they can get their minds back on track by using mental fitness skills.

Be aware of three things when taking mental inventory: the physical body, your feelings, and your mind. Messages from the physical body include sweaty palms, increased heart rate, red face, shaking legs, and tight hands. Messages from feelings are anger, fear, calmness, helplessness, depression, and frustration. Messages from the mind would be lack of focus, negative thoughts, not staying in the now, and doubt. This is taking mental inventory, and observing this information is the first step to mental fitness.

Important Points

1. Taking inventory is the start of changing what's going on inside of you.
2. Change the way you think and feel, and you're on your way to becoming a seasoned hitter.
3. The mind and body are closely connected. Control the mind, and you'll control the body.
4. The professional hitter uses positive self-talk to get focused; this allows him or her to master the body.
5. You must recognize messages you are receiving from your body, your feelings, and your mind. When taking inventory, you must develop active awareness. Active awareness simply means being alert to how you are feeling at any given time.

Active awareness has three steps.

1. Step back, slow down, and observe what's going on inside of you. This first step clears the mind and allows you to be creative.
2. Make a choice and decide what you need for your body to work as you want.
3. Act—do something to adjust, or correct what's going on inside you.

As an example, sometimes before or during an at bat, you may feel lethargic. By being aware of this, you can pump yourself up. At other times you will need to gear yourself down because you may be too excited. The important thing is to observe how you feel, choose what you need to do, and act on those decisions.

This process of observe, choose, and act doesn't apply only to the physical, it applies to what's going on in your mind. If you observe that you're out of focus or tight, you must change this before you hit. If you are doubting yourself, you must use positive self-talk before you get in the box. Until you become aware of how you feel and what's going on in your head, you'll never reach your full potential. When you start to understand and put into practice the "observe, choose, and act" principle, you are on your way to becoming a seasoned hitter. If you do not, you may become your most potent adversary.

To change and control how you feel, you will need to learn and perfect the following skills.

1. Optimism—The ability to think positively at difficult, challenging times
2. Imagery—The ability to see yourself succeeding
3. Energy management—Not getting too high or too low
4. Vision—Being able to see yourself succeeding in the future
5. Attention skills—The ability to focus
6. Mental preparation—Being ready mentally by using positive self-talk

Optimism is looking for an opportunity in difficult, challenging situations. One such situation might go like this: It's the bottom of the ninth, and the score is tied. The best pitcher in the league is on the mound. The opportunities are that you have a chance to put your ability against theirs, and you have a chance to win the game. You must tell yourself this is competition at its best, this is exciting, and this is where you want to be. You have trained your swing and body for this moment. Why throw all that work down the drain with anything but an optimistic mindset?

A positive mental attitude is the most powerful asset a hitter possesses. The baseball season is a long, grueling grind. The hitter who has the ability to forget bad performances is well on his or her way to becoming an optimistic person.

Here is an example of how an optimistic person and a pessimistic person might view the same situation. The situation is this: You have had three bad games, and the third game ended with a strike-out. You are now zero for your last twelve at bats. The pessimistic person might talk in statements like this: "Boy, I've lost it. I can't hit anymore. That first pitch of my third AB was right there. How could I have missed it? Another couple of bad days, and I'll be 0–20 and on the bench."

The optimistic person might think like this: "I've had a couple of bad days, but even the best hitters have them. I remember George Brett had an 0–25 streak once. It's a long season. I've got to realize I'm not going to hit well all the time. The important thing is to keep a good, positive attitude. Tomorrow I'll make some adjustments and get back on track."

Optimistic people perceive their problem as a challenge, as something they can correct. They also see the problem as a way to increase their knowledge of hitting. They learn from their mistakes and know they will make themselves better in the long term. Players who approach a bad game or series of bad games with the proper attitude give themselves a better chance to succeed the next day. Remember, you are always preparing for the future. The past is over, and you can't bring it back.

Those who are not blessed with an optimistic attitude can learn it. But before they take the time to learn it, they must understand its importance and benefits. You must realize all great accomplishments, whether in the business world or on the athletic field, are done by positive, optimistic people. Once you understand how important it is to be optimistic, you are ready to learn an important new skill. The skill is called reframing.

Reframing is taking any situation, especially a negative one, and choosing to focus on the opportunity of that situation. The frame in the word *reframing* is the perception we bring to the situation. We can't often control events that are happening to us, but we can change the way we see those events.

One situation might be that you are in a terrible slump. It is the ninth inning, and the winning run is on second. Where is the opportunity in this situation? That is the question we ask ourselves in order to reframe. Naturally, you would rather be going to the plate coming off a 4–4 streak, but you are not. So if you want to have a quality at bat and have a chance to drive in that run, you had better focus on the opportunity. If you focus on the fact that you are not feeling good, your chances of succeeding go down. You have to pump yourself up and get very determined.

It is not easy to perceive opportunity in tough situations. It takes a level head, imagination, creativity, and character to think positive at difficult times. The opportunity in the above situation may be to learn to relax and face a tough situation head-on and have a quality at bat. Learn to believe in yourself, even if you are having a tough time. Learn to develop character for similar situations in the future. Choosing to focus on positive thoughts and feelings allows your body to relax and perform.

One of the most common ways of sabotaging an at bat is talking to yourself in negative ways. Sometimes this happens when you are in a bad streak. Either before you go to the plate or in between pitches, your self-talk should be what you want, not what you don't want. Your thinking must be, "I want to get a hit," or, "I want to hit the ball hard." If you think it and believe it, you are halfway there. If you don't, you are leaving your at bat to chance.

When you are going well, the process of positive self-talk and confidence building naturally happens. But when you are struggling, it is very important for you to constantly be aware what is going on in your mind. If your mind is racing with negative thoughts, you have to change them before you hit. Don't let your mind control you. Control your mind.

Positive self-talk starts in the dugout. It starts with observing the pitcher and developing your plan. What type of movement does the pitcher's breaking ball and fastball have? Is the pitcher throwing both pitches for strikes? If he or she is not, what is the location? Where is the pitcher's release point? Watch the action of hitters ahead of you. This type of preparation is positive. It is the first step to getting your mind together.

Pete Rose had a habit. After he made an out, he would sit on the top step of the dugout rather than the bench. He did this a number of times. When asked why he did this, he said, "Being alone and getting my mind back on the game helps me forget my last AB." The key word here is *forget*. Getting his mind back on the game helped Pete forget the out he had just made. His mind was occupied by the game; thus, it was impossible for the negative process to happen. It is very important to understand that the moment he started observing the game, his negative thoughts were gone. The ending of his negative thoughts, if he had them, began the positive self-talk process.

Another way to stop negative thinking is to talk to a friend or teammate about something other than baseball. There are many other ways to end the negative thought process. What ways can you think of?

Once you have cleared the mind of negative thoughts, you are now able to feed yourself short positive phrases to give you a positive mindset. Here are some possible phrases.

1. I can hit this guy.
2. I am better than him.
3. If he throws me that same pitch, I am going to kill it.
4. Today is my day. I know I am going to get a hit.
5. This guy is mine.
6. I am going to look for his fastball and whack it.
7. This guy is really struggling—now is the time to get him.

8. This guy is not going to get me out.

9. I am relaxed, confident, and in control.

Feeling determined is another way to erase negative thoughts. Being determined puts you on the offense. It will pump you up and give you positive energy.

Remember, what you say to yourself will directly affect how you feel. Thinking negatively will get you feeling bad, and thinking positively will make you feel good. Don't you feel good when someone tells you how good you are? Hearing it from yourself has the same effect, if you do it enough. A good example of this is Muhammad Ali, who said all the time, "I am the greatest." Every time he said it, he reinforced his confidence in himself. Every time he made that statement, that positive thought was ingrained deeper in his mind. There is no doubt Ali had tremendous physical talents, but the strongest part of his body was his mind.

You do not have to go around telling everyone how great you are, but a little positive self-talk sure helps your attitude. The greatest thing about the power of positive thinking is the mind does not know the difference between something imagined and something that is real. The point is imagining being successful has the same effect on the mind as if it really happened. To put it simply, the mind absorbs and stores what you tell it. It also absorbs and stores what it hears from other people. Learn to talk to yourself in a positive way and surround yourself with positive people. If you do, you will be on your way to controlling events affecting your life.

Important Points

1. Active awareness has three steps: observe, choose, and act. Until you learn this principle, you will be a prisoner to your mind.

2. We use active awareness to inventory how we feel.

3. To change and control our attitude, we must learn the following: optimism, imagery, energy management, vision, attention skills, and mental preparation.

4. Reframing is the skill of learning to see opportunities in difficult times and challenging situations.

5. Be your own best friend: learn to talk to yourself in a positive way.

6. Feeling determined puts you on the offensive and erases negative thoughts.

7. The mind does not know the difference between something that has really happened and something that is imagined.

8. Observation can stop negative thinking and clear the mind.

9. Feed your mind positive phrases to instill confidence.

Notes

_____

_____

_____

_____

_____

_____

_____

_____

_____

_____

_____

_____

_____

**Reframing can be used in any sport or anywhere, when you
need to get yourself into a positive frame of mind.**

HITTING DRILLS

This is a pencil drawing of Steve when he played in Little
League. Drawn by Rich Braun, Steve's brother.

The movement of each hitting style and each hitter has control over the style
he or she decides to use. Just like a doctor, coaches can give hitters a prescription
to develop their hitting style. Through repetition, one can acquire and make
the movements of that style become natural. The key is conscious, methodical
repetition, not just going to the cage or hitting off a tee and beating baseballs
without a purpose. The key to perfecting hitting movements is working slowly
and deliberately. It is a progression from dry swings to tee swings, to batting
practice, and finally to the game.

Drills

Problem: Poor Balance in Stance

Drill 1: Jump up and land

Player gets into his stance and jumps vertically while maintaining his stance. When he reaches the ground, he should feel connected to the ground with a solid leg base.

Drill 2: Pushover

Attempt to pushover the player from all angles, front, back, and both sides. Try to surprise him with your push. This will check his stability. If he has stability and balance, emphasize that he is connected to the ground with his feet.

Drill 3: Blind swing

Take a dry swing with eyes closed. The hitter should focus on his feet and legs. He should have a feeling of stability and a solid connection to the ground.

Problem: Stepping in the Bucket and Front Foot Opening

Drill 1: Off-the-plate striding

In batting practice (BP), move off the plate and force yourself to stride toward either shortstop or second base depending which side you hit from. As you do this, the hitter is to feel her lead shoulder and hip staying closed because of the stride direction.

Drill 2: Two-by-four board

Put a four-foot-long two-by-four board behind the hitter's back and lead foot heels. The board is to be pointing toward the pitcher. This makes it impossible for the hitter to stride anywhere but toward the pitcher.

Problem: Overstriding

Drill 1

Cut down the effort or aggressiveness of the swing. This will slow up the pace of the hitter's strides. Start at the same effort as pepper, then go to 50–70 percent and so on until you can reach 100 percent while still striding short.

Drill 2: Lift up and set down

The front foot is lifted up and set down near the same place. The action of the lifting replaces the action of going out toward the pitcher. It is important when doing this drill to have your conscious mind concentrating on the lifting action.

Drill 3: Stride tutor or stride box

The stride tutor is a device consisting of a plastic chain that attaches to each ankle with Velcro straps. Its purpose is to restrict the length of the stride by adjusting the length of the chain. The stride box is a box five feet by three feet that the hitter stands in while hitting. The length of the stride is restricted by an adjustable board that runs the width of the box.

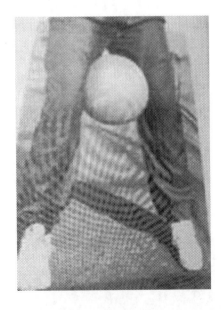

Drill 4: Ball Drill

The hitter holds a ball between his legs just above the knees while taking flips.

Drill 5: No stride hitting

The hitter takes flips and batting practice without striding.

Drill 6: Two concrete blocks

The hitter's lead foot is blocked in with two concrete blocks, one behind the heel and one against the side of the foot. The hitter then hits without striding.

Problem: Uppercutting

Drill 1: Over-the-ball swinging

The hitter takes side or front flips while intentionally attempting to miss the ball by swinging over it. The hitter then progresses to hitting the top of the ball, then to the middle of the ball.

Drill 2: Ground ball hitting

The hitter attempts to hit the ball on the ground.

Drill 3: Target practice

An object is set out in front of home plate fifteen to twenty feet. The hitter takes front flips with the mindset of hitting the object.

Drill 4: Chin to chin

The hitter takes front flips starting with her chin on or near the front shoulder and finishing the swing with chin near the back shoulder.

Drill 5: Double tee

Two tees are used. The first tee, which holds the ball, is placed twelve inches in front and slightly lower than the back tee. The hitter then attempts to hit the ball without making contact with the back tee.

Drill 6: One-knee drill

A. The hitter kneels on her front knee. Kneeling on the back knee causes the back shoulder to drop. The hitter holds the bat with her lead hand and chokes up about ten inches. She then receives side flips, concentrating on pulling the lead arm down and through the swing. It is important to check to make sure the bat barrel is staying above the hands with the hands leading the barrel.

B. Put the top hand on the bat with an open hand. While pulling the bat with the lead arm, use the top hand to push the bat.

C. Two-handed swings concentrating on using the hands only. The hands should stay loose and quick. While doing this drill, feel how the back shoulder stays when the bat is swung with the hands.

Drill 7: Backspin

The hitter takes side flips attempting to put backspin on the ball. The goal is to hit the ball to the back of the cage. If the hitter is putting backspin on the ball, she will feel that the proper way to start the swing is downward.

Drill 8: Hip popper

The hitter starts with the bat behind her back and locked between her elbows. The bat barrel sticks out twelve inches from her body. She then takes side flips while rotating the body and bat barrel down to the ball.

Drill 9: Mound flips

The hitter takes side flips while standing on the downward angle of the mound. The hitter should get the feeling of working her swing down to the ball.

Problem: Long Swing and Casting

Drill 1: Fence swing (dry swings or front flips)

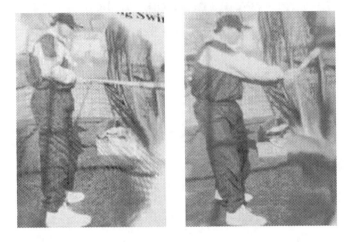

The hitter sets up in his stance standing twenty-four inches to the left or right of fence or cage netting. When he sets up his hands, he should be fifteen inches from the fence or netting. The hitter then takes dry swings or front flips, controlling his early movements. The feeling should be pulling both hands into the slot, which is inside the ball. If the bat touches the fence or netting, the batter is casting the bat barrel.

Drill 2: In-and-out tees

The hitter hits off of two tees. One tee is set on the inside corner, and the other is set on the outside corner. (Important: set on the inside tee up approximately twenty-four inches in front of the front thigh and the outside tee at the front thigh.) A ball is set on both tees. A coach stands behind the hitter, and after the hitter triggers his swing, the coach tells the hitter in or out. The hitter then hits the appropriate ball.

Drill 3: Inside-the-ball tees

Two tees are used. Tee one is set up slightly back and outside of tee two. The ball is set on tee one. The hitter hits the ball while not hitting tee two. This helps to develop a downward swing.

Drill 4: Other-way flips

The hitter takes front flips with the mindset of hitting the ball the other way. The coach flips the ball on the inner half of the plate. Hitting the inside pitch, the other way forces the hitter to keep his hands inside the ball.

Drill 5: Angled flips

The hitter takes front flips from a thirty-degree angle. For a right-handed hitter, the flipper will be thirty degrees to the hitter's right. For the left-handed hitter, the flipper will be thirty degrees to the hitter's left. Balls are flipped to the outside corner, and the hitter goes with the ball the other way. This also develops a swing to hit the breaking ball.

Problem: Cutting Off the Swing

Drill 1: Behind flips

A coach kneels ten feet behind the hitter. The hitter turns her head and faces the coach. She tracks the ball and hits the ball out front with full arm extension. Hitting the ball before it gets out of reach forces the hitter to extend her arms to the front position. After hitting the ball, the bat should continue on the same line from which it was flipped. The coach can control the direction she wants the hitter to hit the ball. To do this, change your angle of the pitch to the hitter.

Drill 2: Out-front tee

The tee is set up slightly more than normal out in front of the plate. This forces the hitter to get her arms fully extended. To keep the hitter from getting out in front, have her hit without a stride.

Drill 3: Double tee

Set up two balls on the tees directly behind each other. The hitter hits through the first ball and hits the second ball. Her mindset is to hit past the first ball to the second. This helps her to feel the bat as well as stay in the strike zone and on the ball longer.

Drill 4: Bat throw

The hitter takes her normal stance and throws the bat up the middle. The release of the bat is made after the arms get fully extended. This will help her feel extension and what it feels like to hit the ball out front.

Problem: Head Pulling

Drill 1: Colored balls

The hitter takes side flips, front flips, or batting practice using colored balls. The object is to track the ball with his eyes and identify the color of the ball.

Drill 2: Finger tees

The coach puts the ball on the tee. As the hitter swings, the coach puts down his finger from one to five. The hitter tells the coach how many fingers he puts down.

Drill 3: Knuckleball flips

The hitter takes side flips with spin. The coach flips a knuckleball, and the object is to identify whether the hitter hit a seam or the white part of the ball.

Drill 4: Hat in front of plate

A hat is placed five feet in front of home plate. Using a front flip only, the hitter tracks and hits the ball. Just after contact is made, the hitter's eyes drop to the button on the cap. This also teaches the hitter that contact is always made from the front high forward.

Drill 5: Head-still drill

The hitter gets into his stance, and the coach puts his hand on top of the hitter's head. While the hitter strides, the coach holds the hitter's head in place. This drill should be done both with the hitter striding long and short to show the hitter the reaction of the head to each stride.

Problem: Loading or Trigger Swing

Drill 1: Golf swing

The hitter takes dry swings using her golf swing. Starting from the address position in golf, swing the bat back to the baseball hitting launch position. This backward swinging action teaches the hitter to load her body weight to the rear leg.

Drill 2: Rhythm system

The purpose of this drill is to give the hitter the feeling that if she shifts her weight back slowly and relaxed, she will approach the ball in the same manner. This creates a rhythm or pace to the striding action. The drill starts with the weight on the front foot (picture 1 below) and the bat hanging forward near the front foot. As the ball is flipped, the hitter drags the bat into the launch position. At the same time, the body weight shifts to the rear leg (picture 2 below). As the bat and weight is shifted back, the hitter immediately strides and swings the bat (picture 3 below). The drill is done slowly and relaxed giving the hitter the feeling she doesn't have to rush or jump at the ball.

1   2   3

Drill 3: Bat throw

The hitter takes her normal stance and throws the bat up the middle. The release of the bat is made after the arms get fully extended. This will help her feel extension and what it feels like to hit the ball out front. (This is the same as in cutting off the swing.)

Problem: Lunging

Drill 1: Stride-separation flips

The hitter receives front flips while separating the swing and the stride. The hitter loads his body weight to his rear leg and then strides while holding his weight back. The ball is not flipped until the stride is completed. Most of his body weight should be back when his front foot touches the ground. The hitter should be in control of his upper body and head. Watch for the head and body floating forward toward the pitcher. This floating action means the hitter is carrying the weight to the front foot too soon.

Drill 2: Fake Flipper

This drill is the same as the stride separation, except the flipper fakes a flip to check the hitter's position after the striding action. The flipper can flip the ball out of the strike zone to work on the hitter's ball strike recognition. This teaches the hitter that it is easier to judge balls and strikes when he doesn't lunge.

Last Message on Drills

These drills will help one learn and perfect the hitting mechanics, but it takes dedication and practice. The desire to improve must be instilled in the youth as early as possible. Use these drills and words of encouragement to help the hitter build confidence and determination. The drills will also help see the ball better to help with strike zone discipline. You will both come away feeling rewarded knowing that you're working to become better.

Notes

Rich Bob and Steve

THE BROTHERS

This is a picture of Steve, Rich, and Bob before a game at Old
Yankee Stadium. Rich and Bob were able to take turns using
one of Steve's uniforms to shag fly balls during warm-up
and visit the plaques and monuments in center field.

THE BROTHERS' STORY

The three brothers, Steve, Rich, and Bob, grew up in the small town of Titusville, New Jersey, and lived in a place called Washington Crossing, New Jersey. They are the oldest of nine children, four boys and five girls. Steve is the oldest, born nine months and one day before identical twins Rich and Bob. Rich was born ten minutes before Bob and was the heaviest, weighing three pounds fifteen ounces compared with Bob three pounds thirteen ounces.

While growing up, they spent many hours playing basketball and baseball in their backyard and neighborhood. All three played Little League, Babe Ruth baseball, and varsity basketball for their high school. Steve went on to play high school varsity baseball and was drafted after high school. He went on to play fifteen years in the Major Leagues and then was a coach in the minor league for a number of years, as indicated in the story about him, "Becoming a Pro." Rich and Bob went on to play years of slow-pitch softball. All three were successful because they wanted to be good by practicing the game they loved to play. They were always first to practice and the last to leave, and they played the game as if they had a one-run lead no matter the score. This approach helped all three have successful sports careers.

Rich was also a great artist and was featured on covers of national magazines; see the part about Rich. Rich was a pitcher that at one time was one of the best around. If one placed the box the softball came in on the plate, Rich could throw a high arc pitch right into the box.

Their practice field when growing up was an old schoolyard at the Titusville grammar school overlooking the Delaware River. Here is a story, about the old practice field where they practiced with their dad. Bob also used the field to practice with his daughters Kim and Emily and son Rob.

THE OLD SCHOOLYARD

by Bob Braun

Take me out to the old ballfield, echoes on the red bricks of the old school. Hopefully another pro will outgrow the fences that were out of reach not long ago.

Many feet have run across the aged green grass that still makes a good field. There goes another pitch of many buckets of balls that have seen the face of the bat—too many to count.

Years ago, I worked with my brothers and waited for my turn to hit. I can still remember enjoying the practices and having fun. How I've enjoyed watching us all grow living different lives but remaining the same. How proud I am to have them play with my kids.

The field would be proud of the success lived by many laughing children who fell, cried, and loved being free to run on it. They are still here to help me develop the next pro who may come out of the old ballfield.

Some of the things that helped the three become the athletes they became are their work ethic and the competition between them. To help build strength, their father bought a five-spring exercise apparatus that they used every night to build muscles, starting with one spring and moved on to using all five springs.

They also did jumps every night to increase their jumping ability: first reaching the doorway and then eventually touching the ceiling. Their mother always complained about handprints on the ceiling.

Carl, the brothers' younger brother, known as Shark, won the New Jersey baseball state championship his senior year in high school as the shortstop and leadoff hitter. Competition and playing with his older brothers helped him develop his skills. He was called Shark because of the way he gobbled up ground balls at shortstop.

Bob's son Rob was also a great ballplayer. He won the batting title his senior year with an average of .455 and made the All-Area team. This was impressive because his league ended up winning two state championships that year.

Baseball is and has been a big part of the Braun family.

STEVE RUSSELL BRAUN

Much about Steve can be learned by reading the story "Becoming a Pro." The story tells what helped make Steve a professional baseball player, and it could help another ballplayer become a pro.

Steve is presently retired from baseball and currently living near a golf course in Fort Myers, Florida. He has spent enjoying his retirement years traveling around the country and visiting his son, Steven; his daughter, Erin; and his grandchildren.

BECOMING A PRO

by Bob Braun

Pinch hitter deluxe, Doctor Stroke, the trump card. These are some of the names Steve has earned because of his ability to deliver a key pinch hit when a game is on the line. Steve developed his skills as a pinch hitter early in his career when he played in the sandlots as a child.

Many of the other young ballplayers he played with would go to the ballfield because there was nothing else to do or because their parents kicked them out of the house. Steve was different. He went to the ballfield to play baseball. He loved the game, he loved the feeling he felt when the ball made contact with the bat, and he loved being a baseball player.

Steve has said many times, "I don't ever remember not wanting to be a professional baseball player." He knew what he wanted to be at a very young age. He went to the sandlot not to waste time but to practice and develop his skills in fielding, hitting, and running. He went to the ballfield because he loved the game of baseball.

Steve played Little League, Babe Ruth, and American Legion. He also played baseball in grammar school and high school. In every stage of his development, Steve played with a great deal of intensity and worked to improve in the game he loved. He listened to his coaches and watched his fellow players, always willing to learn something and improve his skills.

In 1966, after graduating from high school, Steve was drafted in the eleventh round by the Minnesota Twins. Steve was sent to the Sarasota Twins in Florida, the Twins' Gulf Coast rookie affiliate. In his first year at Sarasota, Steve was anything but successful. He hit only .230 with no home runs.

Steve did not get discouraged but continued to work hard in the off-season. He signed another contract with the Twins and started the 1967 season with the Sarasota Twins. He was assigned to the Twins affiliate that played at Wisconsin Rapids after the Gulf Coast League season was completed.

After Steve's second year in professional baseball, he was drafted into the Army. Getting drafted into the Army may have been the most influential event to affect his baseball career. The Army matured Steve, changing him from a boy to a man more determined to achieve his goal of becoming a professional baseball player. He was lucky enough to be stationed in Germany, where he was able to play baseball. In his second year in the Army, he was named the all-star shortstop for the All-Europe Championship baseball team.

Steve was discharged from the Army on September 23, 1969. He played semipro before he went to play winter ball in Florida. This was when Steve began to show his potential.

Due to his maturity and his increase in self-confidence, Steve used his skills developed during his youth to hit .304. This impressed many because Steve not only hit .304 against the most promising young prospects in baseball, but he achieved it after being out of the Army for only two months.

The following summer, Steve was sent to Lynchburg, Virginia, and had an excellent year. He ended up hitting .279 with 43 RBI and four home runs after a slow start. He was also voted to the Carolina League all-star team. Steve was finally showing the baseball world that he had the tools to be a winner. He never forgot the importance of working hard and learning by watching and listening to others.

He would always be one of the first on the ballfield and the last to leave. Steve learned in the Army that there are people of authority who make decisions, and they must be impressed. He worked hard to impress these people of authority, but more important, he was sharpening and developing his skills. He wanted to be a professional ball player.

During the winter of 1970, Steve was again asked to play winter ball in Florida. He had another impressive season. Steve showed the baseball people that as the competition improved, so did his average.

His performance was so impressive that he was invited to Minnesota's 1971 Spring Training camp. This was an unusual achievement because only the top 40 ballplayers in the entire Minnesota organization were invited to the Spring Training camp, and Steve had played for only Minnesota's single-A minor league team.

In the spring of 1971, Steve had his biggest break in baseball. Rod Carew, the regular second baseman for Minnesota, had dental problems. This provided Steve an opportunity to have more playing time than anyone expected.

Steve responded like the pro he is, exceeding all expectations by hitting .334 in Spring Training and playing a superb second base. He made the Twins' twenty-five-man roster that spring to begin his long and successful fifteen-year major league career.

During Steve's career, he played with the Minnesota Twins, the Seattle Mariners, the Kansas City Royals, the Toronto Blue Jays, and then the St. Louis Cardinals. He played in one American League playoffs with the Kansas City Royals. He also played in the 1982 and 1985 World Series as a member of the St. Louis Cardinals.

Steve walked in the game's winning run in the second game of the 1982 World Series, which pitted the Cardinals against the Milwaukee Brewers. He finished this series with a .500 batting average and drove in two runs, helping

St. Louis beat the Milwaukee Brewers in seven games in what was called the series between the beer capitals of the world.

Steve earned the nickname Pinch Hitter Deluxe because of his uncanny ability to come into the late inning game and deliver a key pinch-hit or earn a base on balls.

During the pennant drive in the 1985 season, Steve hit a pinch-hit two-run homer in the tenth inning to win the game against the Dodgers. This key pinch-hit home run kept the Cardinals a half game up on the New York Mets. The next day, Steve singled in another game-winning run to extend the Cardinals' lead over the Mets to a game and a half. These two key pinch-hits helped the Cardinals win their division in 1985 by only a two-game margin.

Throughout Steve's successful career, he has always been known as a great natural hitter. But it was in the last six or seven years that Steve was able to learn and develop his philosophy of hitting. During this time, Steve came to be known as a player who had the skills and mental ability to come off the bench and deliver a key pinch-hit.

Coming cold off the bench to pinch-hit is one of the hardest things to do in baseball. Just imagine being asked to come off the bench, go to the batter's box, and hit against a pitcher who may be throwing at a speed of a hundred miles per hour. Not only are you going up to the plate cold, but you may not have hit or played in a game for a week or two.

It takes a special, disciplined player who has control of his mind and knows and understands the philosophy of hitting. He must spend extra time in the batting cage to simulate the game, and he must use the time he is waiting to mentally and physically prepare himself. He must realize that the team is the most important thing, and the players must win as a team. He must study and analyze other hitters and know the opposition pitchers. All this is done to kill time and be ready to come off the bench to pinch-hit, usually with the game in a win-or-lose situation. All these qualities can be summed up in two words: Steve Braun.

Steve was only the tenth player in the history of baseball to have had a hundred pinch-hits or more, finishing with 113 pinch-hits. He retired from baseball in sixth place on the all-time pinch-hit list, only three pinch-hits behind Jerry Lynch, who is in fourth place. It is quite an accomplishment considering how many ballplayers who have played professional baseball.

Steve always was and still is a student of hitting. He watched and played with some of the best hitters who ever played the game of baseball. Some of these players include Harmon Killebrew, Tony Oliva, Rod Carew, George Brett, Keith Hernandez, and Jack Clark. He always tried to learn from the great hitters. He broke down the swings of these great hitters to determine why they were so good. He applied what he saw and learned to his swing and his philosophy of hitting.

Steve's MLB career began in 1971 as a third baseman for the Minnesota Twins. In his first year, Steve's batting average was .254, and he was voted to *Baseball Digest*'s Rookie All-Star Team as the best rookie third baseman.

In his second year, Steve hit .289 with 50 RBIs. He also played four positions in the field and had his first of seven consecutive 100-plus hit seasons.

He continued to excel as a player. In 1974, he hit .302 for the season, good for tenth in the American League, and he had a career high of eleven home runs. The following year, Steve had a career high of 61 RBIs while batting .289 for the season.

At the end of the 1976 season, Steve was selected by Seattle Mariners in the American League Expansion Draft. He played two years with Seattle and then was traded to Kansas City Royals for pitcher Jim Colborn on June 1, 1979.

While playing with Kansas City, he set a club record for being on base eleven times in a row. Steve still holds the record for the most pinch-hits as a Cardinal.

Steve ended his professional career with a .271 batting average and had 989 hits during his stay in the big leagues. He retired in 1986, a victim of the reduction of the team's roster from twenty-five to twenty-four men.

After his retirement, Steve was the hitting instructor for the Cardinals before moving on to the Boston Red Sox's and Yankees' minor league. The job of hitting instructor is a position in which Steve was comfortable. He has the ability to communicate with younger ballplayers, and his knowledge helps them relax. By being relaxed, they can apply many of his instructions while hitting in a game.

Steve's success in baseball is contributed to his natural ability and his dedication to making himself better: to never be satisfied, but to reach out to make himself a better hitter as well as a better person. With this self-drive, Steve is ensured success in anything he does because he applies many of his hitting philosophies to his philosophy of life.

This is a picture of our paternal grandmother taking her turn at bat at a family picnic.

RICHARD JOSEPH BRAUN

This is a portion of the story dedicated to Rich in the book *Moral Duty* by Bob Braun. Many of the pictures included in this book are done by Rich.

Rich "Dickaloo"

The following are some art pieces by Richard J. Braun, Steve's younger brother and Bob's twin brother. To honor him best is to let you see his love of life though the beauty of his art.

Rich passed away on November 26, 2013, after a long battle with what was thought to be Alzheimer's or frontotemporal dementia. His passing has left an empty spot in Steve's and Bob's hearts.

This is what was written in a local paper.

Richard J. Braun of Ewing, has been accepted into God's loving embrace on Tuesday, November 26, 2013, at Royal Health Gate of Lawrenceville with his loving wife by his side. Dickaloo as he was affectionately referred to by his family and friends, was born in Trenton on February 9, 1949 and was a lifelong area resident. Dickaloo was a self-taught artist who enjoyed the outdoors, fishing, and playing softball with his brothers. He was an avid Yankees fan and sports enthusiast who cheered on Notre Dame football and Duke basketball. Dickaloo loved the beauty of life which inspired him to create art.

Color pencil drawing Rich did of his oldest daughter, Liz. He also has another daughter, Alex. Alex is presently playing on a travel softball team in her area.

Both of these oils are of the Delaware River at Washington Crossing, New Jersey, where in 1776, George Washington and his loyal men crossed the river on a cold Christmas night on their way to independence. The fisherman in *A Good Day* is just south of the bridge shown above.

Both of these drawings are pencil, and each tells a story. Togetherness and love will eventually win, but it is always easier with good memories.

This is an oil painting of our father and his horse, Tu-Down, just prior to a race.

This is a pastel on velvet showing a young girl with her best friend at Christmas.

This is a color pencil drawing of a young ballplayer getting ready to step to the plate. It is in the story "Becoming a Pro" and the cover of this book.

These are color pencil drawings by Rich.

These are oil paintings by Rich.

Taken September 11, 2002, at the Newark YMCA when it was unveiled. It is a large oil painting that has the word "Love" hidden throughout the painting.

ROBERT MARK BRAUN, SR.

A year after high school, Bob was drafted into the Army infantry and was sent to Vietnam, where he was severely wounded in ground action. He is a disabled Vietnam veteran who received two Purple Hearts and a Bronze Medal for bravery, and he was awarded the New Jersey Distinguished Service Medal.

After he was released from the Army, he graduated from Rider College, New Jersey, with a bachelor of science in commerce and a minor in accounting in February 1977. He then worked for thirty-four years as an auditor for the New Jersey State Treasury Department, specializing in inheritance and estate tax. He has been retired since May 1, 2010.

During this time, he self-published the first addition of this book in 1996 and the book entitled "A Story of Life" in 2000. He had to give up marketing the books because he had to raise his children as a single parent. He had to make a choice between his books or children; it wasn't a hard choice, and he chose his kids.

Bob coached and managed his son, Rob, and his daughters, Kim and Emily, for their basketball, baseball, and softball teams. He studied Major League coaches Steve played under, and they all helped him develop his philosophies for his writings on the art of coaching. After retirement, he worked on and completed the second edition of this book and is completing his third book entitled, "Moral Duty."

The best way for you to know Bob is to read some of his stories. Hopefully you have already read the story about Steve in "Becoming a Pro" and "The Old Schoolyard," have read about Rich, and have reviewed his art that showed his love of life. The following story is about Bob's first year of being Mr. Mom. This story is followed by the poem titled "Beauty."

LOOK WHO'S WEARING THE APRON

by Bob Braun

I'm a middle-aged jock who is in my second year of being Mr. Mom, changing positions with my ex-wife by taking over primary physical custody of two minor children. No big deal; it's happening more and more often in today's world of the nineties, where men are accepting the responsibility of caring for their children.

My story starts on December 15, 1993, by moving back into the marital home after over two and a half years of living in a one-bedroom apartment and being an every-other-weekend parent. I had high expectations of molding my kids into highly efficient, on-time machines. I was so sure of my persuasive skills that I totally overlooked the fact that I was dealing with a twelve-year-old boy and a nine-year-old girl. I entered a new life with confidence, believing the household would be running smoothly in a very short time, and I was determined to change things by making my home a perfect environment.

As a morning person who normally got five or six hours of sleep and was in great shape, I saw the everyday responsibilities of washing clothes, doing dishes, and preparing meals as only a slight inconvenience of my routine. I couldn't imagine myself becoming discouraged or sorry about becoming a full-time single parent. There's no way I was going to allow two little kids to stop me from reaching my goals.

While growing up in a large family, I watched my mother labor over a scrub board or old wringer washing machine, washing diaper after diaper for nine children. I was confident that I could manage only two kids in a home with all the modern conveniences of the nineties. I'd survived the Army and the jungles of Vietnam, so I believed there would be no problem training two out-of-control kids.

It was unbelievable that after only three months, I knew what it meant by the saying "Being a mother is a thankless job." I abandoned my belief that the kids would be easily molded into self-efficient, responsible kids. Instead, I was rudely awakened to the fact that any change would take time and a lot more patience than I knew was possible.

I found out what dishpan hands were all about. I also came to understand that for some reason, there are always dishes in the sink, and that the dryer eats socks—not both socks, but only one of a matching pair. I continued to try, after folding the clothes, to match the single socks with the ever-growing bag of matchless socks, and I have experienced the joy of finding a match. It easily overshadows the joy of catching a winning touchdown or hitting a game-winning grand slam—things I used to think were so important.

I quickly gave up my ideology of using my concept of allowance as a manipulating tool to get my two kids to do their chores, make their lunches and beds, and be nice to each other. Instead, I found myself doing exactly what I used to criticize my ex-wife and mother for doing: simply doing things myself instead of battling the kids. It was easier doing things myself than trying to make them do it, but damn it, I knew it was wrong.

I don't know why, but I kept hearing myself say things I'd never accepted before, like "I'm tired of doing everything," "You kids had better start appreciating what I'm doing for you," and "You guys had better start helping because I can't do it all myself." I think that the fumes from the dish and laundry detergent were affecting my brain cells, causing me to lose my power. Maybe it was the sudden change in temperature between sticking my head in the refrigerator and standing over the hot oven. Possibly it was the dust of the vacuum cleaner and the lint from folding the clothes. Whatever it was, it was hard to distinguish the difference of being a Mr. Mom from being a mom. Sometimes I go to the bathroom and stand up, just to remember that I'm not a member of the so-called weaker sex.

I've become aware of how little I appreciated a mother's job: the never-ending amount of responsibilities, chores that must be done every day, and making sure everyone else's needs are taken care of before tending to your own. The stress of planning and then cooking meals that will be eaten, making sure everyone has clean clothes to wear, cleaning, and all the other jobs around the house—it's a job that's never done!

I did have a few things going for me, like a great drive to succeed and an appreciation of life. I learned these things while fighting in the jungles of Vietnam, where I had to fight for my life, plus the loss of my closest friend while serving there. Every day I think about my experience in Vietnam and what my mother went through, and I use them to inspire me to continue to better myself, work hard, and treasure what I have.

There was no way I was going to abandon my goals of teaching my kids the need to learn and take care of themselves. There was no way I was going to admit failure and give up. Lucky for me, I was already doing some things right.

Each weekend, a dish or two was prepared for a quick meal during the week, and there was always homemade spaghetti sauce for a pasta dish. Meals the kids liked were made so they would become confident with my cooking. Fatty foods or sweets were not found in the house, and ready-to-cook hamburger patties were mixed from ground turkey and lean hamburger meat and went into the freezer.

At least one load of laundry was done almost every night, so it wouldn't be a major job. Most of my social life was doing things with the kids, and free weekends were spent cleaning the house, working in the yard and gardens, and remodeling the home. Probably the smartest thing I did was start talking to women, ask them how they managed their home, and then bring up my problems. Gradually, I began to pick up little bits of information to help me run my household.

Every night, I picked up to make sure the house was in order before going to bed. I made sure the two kids did the few chores I assigned, was persistent in making sure they maintained proper sleeping habits, and seldom wavered in making sure we all stayed on schedule. Slowly routines were set and habits were formed, and both kids started losing weight. My son started to swim without a T-shirt because he was no longer embarrassed about extra weight. I started receiving compliments on how much better the kids looked and behaved.

What helped most was enjoying the little victories, like being able to express my love, tucking them in each night, telling them I loved them, and hearing them respond that they loved me too. I told my kids that I was only human and make mistakes just like they do. We started to work as a team, and I learned what motivates them. There were big enjoyments too, like my son excelling in baseball and learning to work hard to improve, my youngest daughter's self-improvements, and developing a closer relationship with my older daughter.

My youngest daughter had a learning disability, so she was struggling in school. She was very cold toward me. I spent time with her and made sure she got into a habit of doing her homework as soon as she got home from school.

Every night I would check her homework, and if it wasn't correct, I would insist that it was done correctly.

Now she does her homework without me telling her, leaves it out for me to check, and doesn't complain when she has to correct a mistake.

Her confidence grew, and she began feeling proud of herself. She has done so well that she has been on the honor roll the first and second marking periods and got straight A's the third. I couldn't have been prouder. My patience and persistence of showing her love has melted the ice between us. She is involved in sports and is a happy, lovable young lady, always ready for a hug and kiss.

My son had already been a good baseball player, and we spent many hours working on it and setting up a weightlifting program for him. He hit off the tee almost every night. By the time the season opened, we were both aware of how much he had improved.

The baseball team he played on, and which I coached, had come in last place the previous two years. The league was the strongest it had been in a long time with no dominating team.

What a year our team had. We went from last to first, winning the playoffs with a record of 17–1. My son hit close to .800 and had a pitching record of 12–1.

I went on to manage the twelve-year-old all-stars. The team won the district championship and came in second and third in two other tournaments. My son was one of the top players, batting third and catching when he wasn't pitching.

Making it through the first year was a major accomplishment. I am now confident in my ability as a Mr. Mom, and I'm sure I'll be able to succeed in caring for my children. I am making sure the house is clean while still maintaining a full and part-time job. I coach baseball and basketball, write, help the kids in school, and do many other jobs around the house. Many nights I go to bed tired, but there is always a smile on my face knowing I've created a stable, happy, and loving environment for my children. I now know that a mother's job is never done, and I appreciate what it takes to be a single parent in the nineties.

BEAUTY

by Bob Braun

Life is beauty.

Each day begins and ends with an array of colors

across the sky.

We wake from the darkness of sleep to the colors of life to love, learn, grow, and

be happy.

Life gives us the ability to share our smiles and overcome the obstacle of living.

Appreciating each day and striving to improve is the essence of the beauty of life.

Health is beauty.

Strength, conditioning, diet are parts of health.

Life is finite, but its quality hinges on the ability to

perform the tasks of life.

We must all strive to maintain ourselves and family by becoming aware of

and then living a healthier way.

The beauty of good health is it can be achieved.

Education is beauty.

Education is learning.

Learning is growth.

It's a process that should never end.

The ability to learn is installed in all of us.

The beauty of education is it can happen anywhere, anytime, at any age,

as long as the desire to improve is a way of life.

Family is beauty.

The foundation of life begins with family.

It's a must if the human race is to live on.

Parents are given the opportunity to pass on love, sharing, kindness.

It starts with patience, setting a good example, and showing love.

A strong family means a strong future—that is the beauty of family.

WHAT IS SAID ABOUT HITTING DRILLS AND MUCH MORE

Babe Ruth Bullpen

***Babe Ruth Bullpen* (September 1997):** *"Hitting Drills and Much More*, a 52-page book that, as the title implies, is much more than just a manual designed to help correct many common hitting mistakes like stepping in the bucket, over-striding, and lunging. It also provides valuable information regarding the development and management of ballplayers. *Hitting Drills and Much More* is a book about keys to success."

Mike Molaro, *Hopewell Valley News*: "A book that makes people feel good about life—themselves. Enjoy the sunrises and sunsets, take time to sit back and relax, appreciate quality family time, slow down, and admire the beauty around us. That's where the "Much More" in the title comes from."

The book "Hitting Drills and Much More" has been increased to one hundred twenty-one pages. The book includes a story about Steve ("Becoming a Pro"), "The Old School Yard," Rich and his art that showed his love of life, and the story about Bob's first year of being Mr. Mom, "Look Who's Wearing the Apron."

OTHER WRITINGS BY BOB BRAUN

MORAL DUTY

The upcoming book is a collection of short stories, other writings, with a few poems wrapped around three stories about Vietnam that were published in a national magazine. Topics range from surviving the jungles of Vietnam, raising three children as a single parent, and losing an identical twin brother. The book includes stories titled "Equal Employment for the Disabled," "Look Who's Wearing the Apron," "The Importance of Amino Acids", "Dementia/Alzheimer", "Flat Tax not Fair", "King's Puppets", "The Nurse the Giver" and stories about cancer, autism, givers, and greed. All these stories are in chapters titled "Moral Duty/Moral Responsibility", "Power of The Pen", "Diet and Health", and "The Love of Life".

These are samples of writings from the book **Moral Duty**.

Blue
Marble

We
have not been
thrown out of the garden
but into it to enjoy the beauty of life.
Where else would you find
a blue marble
in the
vastness of space growing food
right out of the ground?

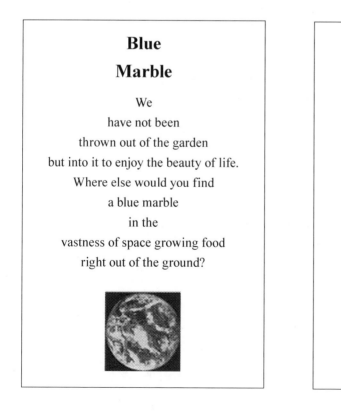

Soldier Boy

Waste, waste, young soldier boy
never return the same,
nightmares of human carrion
Like maggots eating flesh of
Boys ripped from wombs of home.

Heroes lined in black plastic bags,
numbers for each night.

Protest at Kent State
Washington advance
the cause of truth.

Let the souls beyond the
graves protect our
future youth.

WITH ME STILL

"With Me Still" is one of three stories, with "Sun at Last" and "Top of the World, Ma," published in a national magazine, along with a fourth story about Vietnam called "The Bob Hope Show."

The date was March 31, 1970. I had been in Vietnam for almost four months, stationed with the Second battalion, Twelfth Infantry, Twenty-Fifth Infantry Division. It was early morning, and my platoon was on the chopper pad, waiting to be flown out to the jungle for a sweep-and-destroy mission.

My platoon was the last of the company to be picked up for this mission. The other two platoons had been flown out earlier to set up. We were the pushers. Ideally, we were to push the Viet Cong into the other two platoons. The Viet Cong were supposed to hear us, run away, and then be ambushed by our main force as they disappeared into the jungle.

We sat on the chopper pad that morning, and all of us were in good moods. It was payday, and it was supposed to be an easy mission. We had just gotten back from a week in the bush and would have some money and time to relax after completing this assignment.

I sat on the LZ and talked to the squad's radioman, Lt. Sparks, and Jack, with whom I had developed a close friendship. We volunteered to share the point position for the first squad and had walked it for almost two months. We worked together like a well-oiled machine and quickly became the best in our company. He would look for booby traps while I searched the trees for snipers and checked for booby traps, two working as one.

We were dressed in jungle fatigues and fully armed with hand grenades and ammo. A number of us had M-16 rifles. Two men carried M-60 machine guns, one for each squad, with Brownie in mine. A few others were armed with M-79 grenade launchers. We did not pack our normal load of food and water because we were expected to be back later that day.

As we sat there, our radioman cautioned Jack and me to be careful. He told us that he had received reports that the enemy had been spotted in the area we were being flown into. But Jack and I still did not expect to see the Viet Cong.

We heard helicopters in the distance. Soon four choppers appeared. They quickly descended, banked right, and landed on the LZ. Dust flew as Lt. Sparks and the radioman climbed into one side of the first chopper. Jack and I followed. We always sat in the doorway, our feet hanging out the door, ready to be the first ones out. Everyone was quiet as the chopper lifted off the LZ and headed into the jungle. We made a hard left turn, and I held on tightly, remembering the time Jack had grabbed me as I was sliding out of the chopper.

As I sat looking down at the treetops, thoughts of my family ran through my mind. My family was large at nine children, five girls and four boys. I was the third, born nine months and one day after the oldest boy and ten minutes after my identical twin brother. This was my first time away from home, my family, and my twin. I spent the hours and days in Nam trying to picture what they were doing back in the States. The hardest thing was being away from my twin; it was like a part of me was missing.

As I look back, I see that my friend Jack had taken my brother's place in my life. He was a lot like my twin: tough, determined, hardworking, unafraid to stand up for what he believed, and most important compassionate. Jack and I developed a friendship and closeness that I will cherish for the rest of my life.

It took about ten minutes for us to be flown to our drop-off point. As the choppers began to move closer to the treetops, Jack and I began to scan the area for any signs of the Viet Cong. On a previous mission, smoke was spotted coming from a hedgerow. The squad had dropped in on Viet Cong preparing their breakfast. One, who did not disappear fast enough, never ate that breakfast—or any other.

As the choppers flew low, skimming the treetops, they made a lot of noise to signal the Viet Cong that we were there. We were soon dropped off and split into two squads, with Jack and me leading the first.

As we prepared to move out, the radioman again cautioned us to be careful. Jack and I were confident but concerned, and we told the radioman not to worry.

In the past, almost every time we moved into a suspected Viet Cong stronghold, the enemy had gone. They would slip into the jungle or disappear through their complex tunnel system. Our most successful method of destroying our enemy was night ambush, where we sat at night and waited for them to walk into our trap.

But as of late, there had been an increase in enemy activity in the territory we now patrolled. About two weeks before, one of our helicopters was shot down, seriously injuring one of the crew. Also, an out camp on top of a mountain that my platoon had just spent two weeks on had been shelled with 45 mortar rounds.

The new region was thick jungle and bush. We had just taken over the area from the Big Red One and spent a lot more time out in the boonies on patrol. Luck had been on our side: we had not seen any action. But we all knew that it was just a matter of time before our luck changed.

We started cautiously down a well-used trail, with thick jungle on both sides. Jack led, with me close behind. I scanned the tree line for snipers and other signs of Charlie. We proceeded very slowly, all senses on red alert, expecting to be confronted at any moment but hoping that the enemy would flee as was usual. After walking for a little while, we came to a point where the trail branched off to form a Y. The area was scary. The air smelled of Charlie.

Just before the squad reached the Y, Jack and I moved back to the lieutenant and asked him which trail to go down. Lt. Sparks told Jack to check out the trail that branched left, and I was to check the right branch.

I started off, my senses ringing like a five-alarm fire. I thought about what my father had told me just before I had left for Nam: he did not want a hero; he wanted his son back. I checked for signs of recent activity. My past experiences in the woods and fields around my home as a kid had taught me how to tell whether footprints were fresh. While moving down this trail, I saw many footprints that looked very fresh. I thought, *Shoot to kill.*

I came to a small opening in the jungle. That was when I spotted a sandal. It was the type used by the Viet Cong. I knew how important the homemade footwear was, so whoever had been wearing it might still be around. I looked around the opening for other signs of the Viet Cong and then quickly returned to the squad with the sandal to report my findings.

Jack and the lieutenant agreed with me: the right branch of the Y should get a second look. We cautiously returned. Sweat poured off of me. The sun was now high in the cloudless sky. It was hot and steamy, and tension was high. Our earlier confidence had turned into shaky hope that we would survive.

Jack and I crept down the right branch toward the opening. Charlie had been there or might still be there. The air smelled of fish and smoke, a sure sign the area was being used by the enemy. We were a short distance ahead of the rest of the squad, our M-16s on semiautomatic and in the ready position. We warily inched forward but saw no signs of Charlie except for fresh footprints.

Suddenly, about one-third of the way into the opening, Jack and I heard a strange noise: a crack that sounded like a round being chambered or a bullet flying overhead. We hit the ground at the same time and fired our M-16s toward the front left side of the opening. The VC had not run this time; they were there waiting. We'd almost led our squad into a Viet Cong ambush.

There was no cover and nothing to hide behind. We were sitting ducks. Bullets hit all around us, shooting up puffs of dust as they hit the ground. I was on the ground a few feet behind Jack on his right side and shot my rifle into the jungle, hoping I was firing at the unseen enemy. The rest of the squad was behind us, also firing into the jungle and trying to move up to help us.

Jack rolled over on his left side, a hand grenade in his right hand. He looked at me and gave me a smile—the one he always flashed when things got tough. As he threw the grenade, I felt a sharp burning sensation in my right biceps. I looked down to see a small hole in the sleeve of my jungle fatigues. I watched the color of my fatigues quickly change from green to red, and I called for the medic.

At about the same time, Lt. Sparks shouted, "Grenade!" I instantly dove to my right, not really knowing where the grenade was. I never felt myself land. Instead, I was floating in darkness with a bright light in the distance. Everything was peaceful as I moved closer to the light, drifting. I began to think about my family and my twin and how much I would miss them.

I fought hard and regained consciousness. My medic was working on me, trying to stop the bleeding. I had shrapnel wounds in my legs, back, groin, and head, and a bullet wound in my right arm. My head injury caused me to drift in and out of consciousness as I fought the hardest fight of all: the one for my life.

Jack wasn't so lucky. That smile he gave me was the last time I ever saw my friend. Our friendship over the four months we were together, in extremely hard and dangerous times, has left an impression on me that drives me. Many, many times I have asked why I was given the gift of life and not Jack.

Once back in the states, I was able to obtain Jack's home address in Iowa, and I wrote to his parents. I received a couple of letters from Jack's father. He told me how hard Jack's mother and family had taken the loss of Jack, because he was their only child. He explained that their home was in a small town of about 3,200. He went on to tell me that Jack was a good son, that he always brought his friends and girlfriends home to meet his parents, and that his former classmates still made a point of stopping by.

Almost every day, I think about my lost friend and use his image to inspire me, to help me overcome the physical and emotional scars of Vietnam. It is partly my memories of Jack that help me strive to better myself and to encourage and respect others—human traits that we all should practice. I hope that someday, boys like Jack, me, and many other young Americans will never be ripped from their wombs of home to fight a senseless war like the one in Vietnam.

Dedicated to Jack Rae Smith

The following is written on the Vietnam Memorial in Washington, DC.

Smith, Jack Rae

SGT-Army Selective Service

25th Infantry Division

20 years old, single, Caucasian, male

Born 04/18/49

From Clarion, Iowa

His Tour of duty Began on 11/26/69

In Dinh Duong, South Vietnam

Ho Stile, Ground Casualty

Multiple Fragmentation Wounds

Body was Recovered

Religion

Church of Christ.

Panel 12W Line 63

Visit my friend

Printed in the United States
By Bookmasters